FAMILIA

Los Castellanos in San Diego, 1906
Left to right, standing: Ramona, Jesus, Abel; middle row: Narcisso,
Cleofas holding Tiburcio, Francisca; front: Juana and Espiridiona.

FAMILIA

MIGRATION AND ADAPTATION IN BAJA AND ALTA CALIFORNIA, 1800–1975

Robert R. Alvarez, Jr.

Foreword by Renato Rosaldo

UNIVERSITY OF CALIFORNIA PRESS

Berkeley · Los Angeles · Oxford

University of California Press
Berkeley and Los Angeles, California

University of California Press, Ltd.
Oxford, England

First Paperback Printing 1991

Library of Congress Cataloging in Publication Data
Alvarez, Robert R.
  Familia: migration and adaptation in Baja and
Alta California, 1800–1975

  Bibliography: p.
  Includes index.
  1. Mexican American families—California.
2. Family—Mexico—Baja California. 3. California—
Foreign population. 4. Baja California (Mexico)—
Social conditions. I. Title.
F870.M5A6   1986   979.4'980046872073   85-23217
ISBN 0-520-07389-4 (alk. paper)

Printed in the United States of America

2 3 4 5 6 7 8 9

The paper used in this publication meets the minimum requirements of
American National Standard for Information Sciences—Permanence of Paper
for Printed Library Materials, ANSI Z39.48–1984. ♾

To the memory of my grandparents
Adalberto Smith
Dolores Salgado
Ramona Castellanos
Ursino Alvarez

and for
Luis, Mollie,
Lankfie and Corey,
and the children who follow

CONTENTS

4

Calmallí: The Mining Circuit and Early Network Development, 1880–1910   50

5

San Diego and Calexico: The Frontera and Early Network Formalization   95

6

San Diego–Lemon Grove: Florescence, 1930–1950   118

CONTENTS

7
Epilogue   151

8
Conclusion   162

Appendix:
Original Spanish Field Notes   173

Notes   185

Bibliography   193

Index   203

MAPS

PHOTOGRAPHS

FOREWORD

Familia seriously revises the picture of Mexican immigration developed in previous studies. True to its title, Robert Alvarez's book traces the diffuse enduring relations that connect members of his own extended family over a century of the remembered past. Through crisscrossing alliances of marriage and *compadrazgo* his family network grows stronger rather than declining over time.

Studies that focus on one point in time or analyze individuals rather than familial networks fail to see the historical patterns of loosely coordinated movement that Alvarez so convincingly delineates. His familia moves through time and space like a caravan on a meander, now moving northward then southward, rather than like a series of individuals moving once and for all from Mexico to the United States.

Alvarez's study suggests that the very notion of the border needs reconceptualization. Other studies lead readers to imagine waves of people crossing the border through a one-way tunnel, never returning and never looking back. In *Familia,* however, the border appears as an increasingly inconvenient barrier to processes that transcend it. His familia inhabits a region that extends on both sides of the border. Binational linkages shape patterns of migration, economies, and identities for family members.

Familia invites its readers to imagine the border as a busy intersection where traffic moves in several directions at once. Although massive inequalities between the United States and Mexico condiiton life along the borderlands, they do not produce a simple northward flow of people and a southward flow of commodities. This is a zone where "Los Smith," as their name suggests, have assimilated an ancestral European American: it is a space marked by processes of both Americanization *and* Mexicanization.

At the same time that this book reconceives the borderlands and presents a fresh analysis of U.S.-Mexican migration, it also reveals a research process that transforms the researcher. Alvarez becomes conscious of how his familial past has shaped his present. His compelling story of self-discovery is more oblique than explicit. When speaking of Ursino Alvarez, he only parenthetically describes him as "my paternal grandfather." When Loreto Marquez describes his late nineteenth-century past in a mining town, he links it to the present: "Life was very hard. Well, in those years there wasn't a thing like today. Uhhh! Today the difference is like heaven" (p. 61). Alvarez discovers and claims his place in a history never before told in textbooks.

When the native and the ethnographer are one and the same person, old practices take on new meanings. Such meanings become even more evident when the present text is considered alongside the films *The Trail North* and *The Lemon Grove Incident* (available through KPBS-TV, San Diego). The first film depicts Alvarez with his son on their journey to recover their history. The second portrays an early desegregation case involving Alvarez's father, mother, and the community settled by familia members. Taken together, the films and the text provide a vivid portrait of a familia, its patterns of migration, settlement in the United States, and its struggles to claim social justice.

Renato Rosaldo
Stanford University 1991

PREFACE
AND
ACKNOWLEDGMENTS

Many individuals helped make this book possible. The most important are the kin and friends who lived this experience and whose history and relationships endured into my own lifetime. Without these folk I would never have attempted to describe and explain the personal and sociological events that inspired in me the deep sentiment and respect I hold for family members and friends. This book tells the story of my own extended family, how they came to settle in the United States and the reasons for their perseverance. In many ways this is a story of individuals and the daily task of living. But the story is set in the context of major political and economic change in the Western Hemisphere which stirred decisions and new expressions of support among a group of Mexican migrants who eventually crossed the United States-Mexican border. The pioneer settlers still alive when I set out to document this history were instrumental in identifying the historical episodes, the variety of social and geographic landscapes, and the means of support they utilized in the journey north. These kin and friends granted me their time and glimpses into their personal lives that formed the basis of this book. Señor Loreto Marquez was a continuing inspiration, for he made the mines of the peninsula and the sentiment of the early pioneers come to life. My great-aunt Martina Mesa de Romero provided me with a descriptive picture of the many families and individuals I had never known. They, like others whose help was instrumental, have passed away, but they live on in the pages of this book. María Smith de Mendoza, Levorio Mesa, María Sepulveda, Refugio Sotelo, and Carlos Mesa are among those who are no longer living. Francisca

Castellanos de Moreno (my godmother), Mercedes Alvarez de Palmer, Tiburcio and Refugio Castellanos, and numerous other kin offered invaluable help and support. Bernardo Hollman, Nicolás Ceseña, and other family friends who came north from the little pueblos of the south were also instrumental in the formation of the picture presented here. My debt to them goes beyond the book because they helped me realize the importance of the people who lived those early days.

I owe the many colleagues and friends who encouraged the research and writing special thanks. At the inception of the study I was faced with a professional dilemma because I chose to study my own family. The questions of personal distance and objectivity could have become a major obstacle, but support from George A. Collier, Renato Rosaldo, Bernard J. Siegal, Benjamin D. Paul, and George D. Spindler made the research, writing, and the final result meaningful in both a personal and professional way. Their scholarly criticism has been a guide and measure to all my work. George Clement Bond and Jerome Wright provided valuable feedback on the early manuscript. Robert Wasserstrom, William and Eva Demarest, Juan Felipe Herrera, Leo Chavez, Levie I. Duran, Ted Gordon, Fred Dobb, and others provided support through the hard times. Valuable suggestions were offered by Edgar Butler, William Davis, and the unnamed reviewers of the manuscript. I am also indebted to my editor, Amanda Clark Frost, whose copy editing and knowledge of Baja California helped produce a more readable and accurate manuscript.

The research would never have been completed without the generous support from the National Institute of Mental Health, the Ford Foundation, the Center for International Studies, and the Department of Anthropology, Stanford University.

My greatest debt, however, is to my immediate family. My mother, María Smith Alvarez, has been a continual inspiration and example whose faith in my work has never faltered. Her energy and outlook have been constant reminders of the necessity of pursuing just causes. Her help in identifying and meeting numerous members of the family network in San Diego and Baja California was invaluable. My father, Robert R. Alvarez, has helped in many ways, especially in conveying the respect he holds for the elders of the family and by exemplifying the uncompromising determination of the settlers who came before us. My sisters, Sylvia Anna and Guadalupe María, have been constant encouragements. George P. Cooper, my brother-in-law, introduced me to the southern peninsula and helped me realize a potential that I am still tapping. Lankford O. Jackson, Sr., left us all a legacy that is a continuing inspiration. In addition, Michael Marcus has continually offered feedback and insight into the worthiness of my work. I am also grateful to Martha and Joel Marcus, who have taken a keen interest in my research and intimately know what the struggle has been.

I owe my wife, Karen Hesley Alvarez, and my children, Luis and Amalia, special gratitude because they lived through the strains of the conceptualization, research, and writing of the manuscript. Karen read, typed, and sensitively commented on every aspect of the book. Without the understanding and help of my family this book would never have been completed.

Although this book represents the collective efforts of these people and others not named here, I alone take responsibility for any errors of fact or interpretation.

INTRODUCTION

This book is about a group of families that migrated north from Baja California Sur and settled along the U.S. border of Alta California. As a child I knew many of these families; indeed my own grandparents and great-grandparents had come from the south. Only recently did I realize that their history and role in border settlement was not only unrecognized but was fading in the minds of their descendants. Stirred by the idea of keeping their memories and accomplishments alive, I decided to reconstruct the history that brought them as migrants to the border and, from my perspective as an anthropologist, to identify the sociocultural patterns of their migration and adaptation.

I have a number of objectives here, but the primary motive is to demonstrate how the institution of the family ensured sociocultural stability as people moved within social contexts that were different from those they had known in their hometowns. As these people moved north the family and its institutions continued to be the principal base for successful adaptation and maintenance of cultural values. Migrants kept in touch with hometown kin, were received and aided by kin throughout their migration north, and extended kin ties to new friends and acquaintances in the course of the journey north. Family institutions provided the social mechanisms for the formation of a large family network that developed along the Frontera when numerous migrants came together there.

This family focus also illustrates how migration can contribute to the extension and maintenance of families over geographic space. Through the migration process families extended kin ties that had their counterparts in southern Baja California. This suggests that in this case migration helped increase family solidarity and family relations rather than causing disruption and breakdown. Families used the migration experience to extend family ties from hometown regions to new social contexts throughout the journey north.

By the late 1940s and 1950s when I was growing up, this group of families had developed into a strong community of kin in which family respect, family support, and family continuity were constant values. These values were expressed and were strengthened through a number of familial-social affairs that included *cumpleaños* (birthdays), *bautismos* (baptisms), marriages, and funerals. The people I remember and the kin ties that brought us all together became a basis for documenting the rich patterns people identified in their movement north and in their settlement along the border.

The description and explanation of how this family network developed is the basis of this book. The earliest group of unrelated families that came north in a stage migration shared a number of common cultural values, including a strong regional affiliation with the peninsula of Baja California. This affiliation and their strong family institutions became the means to express support as the families migrated north. Once in the border region the migration experience itself served as another common bond recognized by Baja migrants. All these common experiences and values became the basis for the multiple extensions of kin among the first pioneer migrants and later groups that arrived on the border.

The actual research for the study was done between September 1975 and January 1977. Working principally in San Diego county, I contacted pioneer migrants and their offspring who had crossed the border around the turn of the century. As principal individuals identified kin and friends, I followed the network in a discovery process that led me to other individuals within San Diego county and various peninsular towns, including Tecate, Ensenada, Maneadero, Tijuana, Loreto, and Comondú. I have supplemented the primary interviews with subsequent trips into Baja California during the last five years. Many of the individuals I interviewed were people I had known as good friends and acquaintances of my own grandparents. Others were names I had heard as a child. I soon discovered that these and other folk I had not known were *parientes* (kin) who recalled specific periods of time and geographic locales as significant factors in the establishment of family ties in San Diego. Their recognition of specific locales at distinct periods of time led to the development of the historical emphasis of the study. I became engrossed in the historical background of family relations and realized that specific periods in the history of the Californias provided the contexts for the twentieth-century migration I was investigating.

The historical context forms more than mere background for the development of the Californio kin network in the United States. The context also includes the socioeconomic and political environments in which the migrants of this study found themselves as they left the little towns of the southern peninsula, entered the mines, and crossed the border and settled in the United States. Current work in anthropology has begun to focus on the explanation of social behavior through analysis of macro- and microlevel influences (see Orton 1984; Davis 1985). The case presented here illustrates the importance of examining not just the historical background of the migration north but also the economic and political conditions that influenced local behavior throughout the migration.

This analytic perspective draws attention to larger conditions in the western hemisphere which affected the families and individuals of this study. Economic conditions changed and fluctuated because of national decisions in Mexico. Major economic developments, such as the growth of capitalistic ventures throughout the west, exploited migrant labor and natural resources in Baja California. Individuals and families made specific choices concerning family and economic security as economic contexts changed; these choices played a role in the development of extended kin ties and the formalization of social relations through marriage and godparenthood. The settlement of the San Diego community was thus a stage in a series of historical episodes, each of which played a role in the expansion of social relations and the final decision to cross the international border.

From a historical perspective the twentieth-century Californio migration is an episode in a long history of mobility in the Californias. Regional mobility and migration in the Californias has its roots in sixteenth- and seventeenth-century exploration of the Pacific Coast; this mobility also encompasses the establishment of the Spanish eighteenth-century settlements that migrants of this study identify as hometowns and locations where families and kin ties were first formed.

In the early Baja California settlements of Comondú, Cabo San Lucas, Loreto, and others, families were first established, and from these towns families moved north along the roads and trails established during the early centuries of Spanish penetration. Some families moved alone but were soon followed by sisters, brothers, and their families. Many followed the boomtown trails into the mines opened in the nineteenth century. Others steamed north to Mexicali through the Gulf of California. And a few walked across the international line to the border towns of Southern California.

As the migrants became part of the peninsula, so the geography became part of them. The country is Mexico: "Soy Mexicano" (I am Mexican), they say. The regional affiliation is to Baja California: "Pero, soy de la Baja California" (But I am from Baja California), they insist.

PLAN OF THE BOOK

This book is organized chronologically, beginning with the sixteenth-century discovery of Baja California and ending with the settlement of the border in the twentieth century. The first chapter emphasizes the role of geography and climate in the initial settlement of California and illustrates the northward orientation of Baja inhabitants which resulted from Spanish exploration in the sixteenth, seventeenth, and eighteenth centuries. Chapter 1 sets the background for the nineteenth-century context in which the migration treated in this study began. Geography is more than a physical barrier that inhibited movement. It is part of the history that became embedded in place-names associated with family background and regional affiliation maintained by border migrants.

In chapter 2 I interpret specific political and economic developments of the nineteenth century as they pertain to family migration. These developments take place in a wider perspective that includes both Alta and Baja California; this context illustrates the economic effects of the continuing patterns of mobility in the Californias. In this context I focus on migration and the simultaneous development of the network. Chapter 3 introduces the developmental sequence of the family network. The three phases of this sequence correspond to stages in the migration north. Chapters 4, 5, and 6 constitute historical reconstructions of each phase, including the social, personal, and local attributes of migration and network development. These chapters demonstrate how families interrelated and used regional ties and a common sentiment toward hometowns and locations where friendships had formed.

The historical-regional framework of this study shows that the northward migration of these families was not an isolated event caused solely by the economic opportunities during a single period of time. Rather, migration, at least in this case and probably for other Mexican migrants, was part of a regional-familial tradition. The Californio migration can be considered a sociocultural response rather than simply a disruptive consequence of poor economies that forced individuals out of hometowns and into the border region.

This book then is a social history of the migration and adaptation of Baja Californios. But it is also an example of the rich diversity in the continuing Mexican migration and settlement in the United States. This study presents a small segment of a larger history of people from other Mexican regions who continue to hold sociocultural ties and who identify with specific towns, regions, and people on both sides of the U.S.-Mexican international line.

– 1 –

THE HISTORICAL AND GEOGRAPHIC BACKGROUND OF MOBILITY

The purpose of a geographic description in anthropological studies is to acquaint the reader with the physical terrain and climatic conditions in which specific human behavior takes place. This is only part of the goal I have in mind here. The individuals and families that are the focus of this study have conveyed, indeed, have instilled in most of their offspring, a regional, familial allegiance to Baja California. The peninsula was the home of their fathers and mothers and the birthplace of the families, like my own, now in San Diego. This deep feeling was produced by the Californios' close ties with the geography and families of the peninsula. They tell stories not only about people and social events but about places in the desert and the mountains and in the hometowns from which they came. To migrants on the difficult desert routes north and south, place-names and geographic particulars acquired special meanings as they became part of social interactions and individual histories.

As geography is tied to the movement of twentieth-century migrants, so too is it intimately tied to early historical processes. Geography and climate in the peninsula were the single barrier that consistently defeated early attempts at colonization. And once colonization and settlement occurred, only unique geographic locales allowed Spanish settlement. The majority of the peninsula was never penetrated. Because of geographic obstacles, roads and paths seemed to develop only in naturally passable areas between early missions and towns. These same paths became wagon roads and main routes between the early settlements in Baja and Alta California. The roads were well but sparsely traveled and in the twentieth century they were the main arteries that connected the migrants of this study to the developing frontier. Peninsular geography maintained a dominant role throughout the colonial period and into the present. In 1972, when the first transpeninsular highway was paved and completed, it followed much of the early route of the original El Camino Real.

THE GEOGRAPHY

Baja California was born about twenty-five million years ago. After quiet millennia the San Andreas fault split California and northwestern Mexico apart, creating the Gulf of California. Although this action was a slow process and continues today, the result was an isolated peninsula, approximately eight hundred miles long, torn away from the motherland some hundred miles across the gulf. As the break came the peninsula was slowly uplifted and tilted. The land became a broad, gentle, rolling plain. The old river systems that had drained across Mexico into the Pacific were cut off and began to flow into the gulf. The creation of the gulf produced current and air pressure systems along the peninsula that increased aridity. Today the peninsula is dependent for rainfall on outside pressure systems in the north and northeast.

The flat alluvial plains and deserts are broken by abrupt, jagged peaks dispersed throughout the peninsula. These mountains have been described as "granite blocks." Deserts and plains have earned the land a reputation for fiery heat and distinctive cactus vegetation. These extremes have forced modern as well as historic travelers in the peninsula to make their way between the peaks and through the deserts—for there was no other way.

Natural historians generally break the peninsula into three regions (Coyle and Roberts 1975; San Diego History Museum 1977; Hendricks 1971), primarily for ease of description. Typically, there are no distinct beginnings or endings of ecological zones. These three zones are the northwestern or frontera zone, the desert zone, and the cape region. Each zone delimits specific flora and fauna as well as specific climatic conditions.

The Northwest: The Frontera

The first ecological zone is the northwestern, often referred to as the frontera in Baja California history. The frontera has always been the northern frontier zone of Baja California. This zone includes the present U.S.-Mexican border region and extends south to El Rosario about 360 miles. It is also called the California region because of its topographical similarity to Southern California. This area consists primarily of the high mountains in the northwest, but the peaks of the Sierra de la Gigante and the range of Las Tres Vírgenes (a recently extinct volcanic chain) are often included because of their vegetation. This zone consists basically of the peninsular range, including the Sierra Juárez and the San Pedro Mártir range. The granite peaks of the north range rise over 5,000 feet in elevation and encompass an area some 160 miles south of the Alta California border. Sections of the Guadalupe and Cedros islands and the west coast strip from San Diego to San Quintín also form part of this region. The major types of vegetation are coniferous forests, piñon and juniper woodland, chaparral, and coastal sage. In the northwest the native Cucupah, Pai-Pai, and Southern Diegueno have forested these regions, and today piñon nuts are collected and sold commercially by families in the mountains.

The Desert

The majority of land on the peninsula is desert. This desert runs the entire length of the peninsula, beginning with the San Felipe Desert on the east side of the northern mountains and extending to the Vizcaíno Desert on the Pacific in a long midsection. The central desert, beginning south of El Rosario, includes the Vizcaíno on the Pacific, branches out toward the Bay of La Paz in the south forming the Gulf Coast Desert, and includes the Magdalena Plain on the west.

The central desert begins just south of El Rosario and ends about six hundred miles south near La Paz. This is a lush desert that boasts rugged peaks and clear, dry skies. The diverse vegetation is generally of low growth, except for the giant cardon and cirio, but it is widely spaced, leaving flat sand surfaces for the zigzagging of travelers. The desert is bounded by the jagged peaks of the Sierra de la Gigante on the southeast. On the west the sandy flats of the Vizcaíno Desert extend to the Pacific Ocean.[1]

Before the arrival of the Spanish in the sixteenth century the central

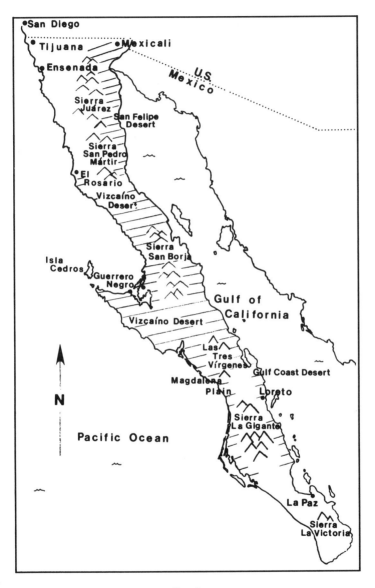

Map 1.
Baja California

desert was the most populated region. Of a total estimated population of 50,000, about 25,000 people lived in the central desert (Aschmann 1967). The early missionaries coerced the native groups into Spanish-style settlements and cut off their balanced pattern of seminomadic foraging. This alteration in life-styles, coupled with the decimation wrought by the introduction of European diseases, resulted in the total extermination of Indians from this region.

The extreme aridity and economic sparseness of the central desert isolated the northern region from the cape. Although the north was settled by Spanish from the south, the central region was passed over (for the fertile north) and left virtually unpopulated. During the mid and late 1800s some gold mining prospects brought small populations of miners from both the north and south into these areas. Once the ore was gone, people abandoned the region. Today small pockets of people live throughout the area in deserted mining and mission spots. Today it is the region least populated on the peninsula.

The Cape

The Tropic of Cancer bisects the cape zone, which begins near Loreto, in scarce mountain forest and fans out to include La Paz and the southern tip of the peninsula. The vegetation there is primarily tropical, although the cardon cactus is still present among lush growth and a variety of tree life. As in the other regions, the mountains—the Sierra La Victoria—are rugged peaks rising to heights of over 7,000 feet.

The towns of the cape are among the oldest in the peninsula, and it is in this region that the Spanish first met their defeat. La Paz was the first site of discovery in 1533 and there in 1535 the first settlement in the Californias was begun. But Indian uprisings and the harsh environment forced the Spanish out. Settlers returned in 1596, establishing the settlement permanently. La Paz, the capital of Baja California Sur, is the gateway to San José del Cabo and Cabo San Lucas, where land's end meets the turquoise water of a tropical Pacific.

THE CLIMATE

The climate, like the geography of the peninsula, made initial settlement difficult for the Spanish. The peninsula was viewed as a hot, arid, and inhospitable frontier in which all settlement relied on imports from the mainland across the gulf. Early as well as modern travelers consistently remark about the peninsular heat, the lack of water, and the vast stretches of desert terrain. The Jesuit Baegert wrote in the eighteenth century:

> If I wished to describe California (of which it is said in jest that of the four elements it received only two: air and fire) in a few words I could say with the prophet in the sixty-second psalm that it is a waterless desert, impassable because of rocks and thorns, or that it is a long rock jutting out of the sea, overgrown with extraordinary thorn bushes, and almost devoid of grass, meadows, forests, shade, rivers, and rain... (Baegert 1772)

Baja California's general location between the Tropic of Cancer and 32° 50' N contributes greatly to the varying climatic conditions throughout the peninsula. The greatest climatic influences are the ocean currents and winds that bring precipitation in varying amounts. Annual peninsular precipitation varies from no rainfall in some localities to thirty inches in the higher mountains of San Pedro Mártir. The California current, originating in the western Pacific, travels north along the coast of Japan, circles across the Pacific around 40° N, then turns south along the west coast of Alta California and Baja California (Schwenkmeyer 1977). It brings cool ocean temperatures (55°–65°F) and produces mild temperatures and frequent fog on the west coast of the peninsula. Because there are no significant mountain ranges on the west, the great plains of Magdalena and the coastal sections of the Vizcaíno Desert are generally cooler than other desert regions, averaging 75°F. The California current dissipates at the cape, where both land and water temperatures are higher.

The cape region receives much of its precipitation from the west coast of Mexico. This comes in the form of tropical cyclones known as *chubascos*, which generally occur in late summer or early fall.[2] Only the cape in the far south, the lushest region on the peninsula, and the mountains of the north receive rainfall that at times exceeds 40 inches annually (San Diego Natural History Museum 1977:2). Cyclonic air masses from the northern Pacific bring winter storms to the northern part of the peninsula, but these rains dissipate as they head south, extending to about El Rosario, a little over 200 miles south of Tijuana. The average annual precipitation in Tijuana and San Diego is 10 inches (8 inches in Ensenada and 5 inches in San Quintín).

The central peninsular desert and the northern cape, north of La Paz, is the country from which early exploratory travelers headed inland and from which twentieth-century migrants moved north. It is the hottest and driest region of the peninsula and has presented the most consistent challenge in all periods of exploration and settlement.

DISCOVERY AND SETTLEMENT

The Spanish quest for discovery and settlement in the sixteenth and seventeenth centuries established a northerly pattern of movement. Although I provide a brief history of the settlement of peninsular mission towns, my primary focus here is this mobility and the lines of communication that became prominent in Baja and Alta California during this period. This movement pattern is embedded in the processes of discovery and encompasses the important events that brought discoverers and settlers to the peninsula and eventually to the Frontera in the eighteenth, nineteenth, and twentieth centuries.[3]

Before discovery California had been a mere legend, fueled by tales recounted by mainland natives. The land was believed to be an island of fabled Amazons in which gold and treasure would surpass all booty taken in previous pursuits. This legend played an important role in the successive attempts at northward expansion, in the discovery of California (named after the legendary queen of the Amazons), and in the persistent, though incredibly difficult, exploration of the gulf and peninsula of Baja California.

When the Spanish, under Cortéz, entered Baja California during the first century of exploration, they met a hostile land that was to defeat many settlement attempts. Yet however poor the economic possibilities and resistant the geography and climate, explorers continued to attempt settlement and colonization on the peninsula. The search for more suitable settlement sites continued, and when the more hospitable lands and coast of Alta California were discovered, Baja California became a migratory way station to the north. Missionaries, settlers, and the Manila galleons skirted her shores as they headed north to Alta California and returned south to New Spain.

The pattern of northward movement eventually left Baja California virtually unsettled and physically unconquered. Exploration had stemmed first from the quest for a western sea passage to the Indies and then from the race for the fabled riches of the new northern continent. Baja was a desolate place that offered ceaseless hardship. Only a handful of missionaries saw this frontier as worthy of time and dedication and they eventually developed the towns and routes that likewise headed north.

The Context of Discovery

Cortéz became the key figure in the discovery of the peninsula because when he heard of the island legend soon after conquering Mexico[4] he became obsessed with its discovery and settlement. He first heard of an Amazon province through the Tarascans, and in 1524 he wrote Charles V of the existence of such a land, rich in gold and pearls, to which Colima natives had traveled. In 1522 (when word reached Spain of Magellan's successful voyage to the Philippines via the southernmost straits of the Pacific), Cortéz ordered his lieutenants west in search of gold mines and a water passage to the South Sea. They explored the isthmus of Tehuantepec (Cristóbal de Olid), Oaxaca (Pedro de Alvarado), and the coast of Guerrero (Pedro Alvarez Chico). In May of that year Cortéz began to outfit and build a fleet that was to be used for an expedition in search of the rich islands off the Pacific coast.[5] But Cortéz had to wait five years before ordering the fleet into the Pacific because the king supported a new expedition from Spain. Charles V hoped to establish a direct route from Spain to the Indies in order to take direct control over the Spanish spice trade. But this expedition was lost and the king issued Cortéz a Royal Order of Pacific Exploration (Schurz 1939:15). Cortéz lost no time and in 1527 sent his cousin, Alvaro Saavedra Leron, on an ill-fated voyage to the Spice Islands. Saavedra was lost in the Moluccas attempting to find a return passage to New Spain, but the expedition had immediate consequences for successive sea exploits. The search for a return route from the Indies became a prime goal in ongoing exploration to counter the Portuguese monopoly of the Indies trade.[6] Spain's immediate hope to take an active part in the trade was to establish a western route via the New World.

The struggle between the major explorers and conquistadores also forced Cortéz out of mainland exploration and into the Gulf of California. In Mexico City the infamous Guzmán, as member of the *audencia,* began using his powers for personal gain, and the viceroy Mendoza attempted to limit Cortéz.[7] Although Cortéz had been issued the royal license to explore and conquer the islands of the Pacific and the unknown coasts of the mainland, Guzmán wrote the king that he (Guzmán) planned to search for the country of the Amazons.

Cortéz, attempting to reclaim what had rightfully been his by earlier conquest and exploration, in 1532 sent Diego Hurtado de Mendoza just north of Guzmán's territory. Mendoza was killed by native Sinaloenses but Cortéz did not give up. In the following year the peninsula was "discovered." Cortéz sent two ships into the gulf, but they became separated early in the voyage, and one managed to land on the peninsular shores. One ship returned to Acapulco and the continuing vessel was seized by Ortuno Jiménez in a mutiny. Jiménez, in 1533, became the first European to sail into the Bay of La Paz and land on the peninsula.

Jiménez received no welcome, and from the outset the peninsula became known as inhospitable country. The mutineering captain and most of his men were killed by natives, but a few men managed to escape to the mainland where they were seized by Guzmán. One survivor escaped, however, and reached Cortéz with news of the discovery of an island rich in pearls and gold (Wagner 1929:6).

When Cortéz learned of the discovery, he lost no time in preparing a follow-up expedition. Cortéz himself commanded this fleet. He set sail in 1535 with provisions for a settlement and entered the present Bahia de La Paz. Baja California again gave no welcome and was to become as isolated as if it had been the island it had always been deemed by the Spanish. The Europeans found the peninsula harsh. There was no prosperous settlement and the colony struggled along until 1537. Then Cortéz found it necessary to return to New Spain to defend his rights of conquest and acquisition and he never again saw the New World. The settlement at La Paz failed and the peninsula was left unsettled for over a century and a half.

This earliest expedition to Baja California as well as those that were to follow in the next century contributed knowledge of sea travel along the gulf. The siting and attempted settlement of La Paz created sealanes that the Spanish continued to use between the cape and the mainland. Furthermore, La Paz became a major harbor from which the Spanish galleons explored both gulf and Pacific. For the next two centuries mobility in Baja California was restricted to the sea.

After Discovery:
Exploration and the Manila Galleon

By the early 1540s, just twenty years after the conquest of Mexico, both coasts of the peninsula had been explored and the northern territory of California was soon to be penetrated. In 1540 Díaz entered western Baja California by land via the mainland route that still stands today. Two years later Cabrillo stood at the Pacific. The principal routes to the Californias had been discovered, but unlike their mainland counterparts, they would not be used for immediate settlement. California remained unimportant except insofar as its coasts could aid in the burgeoning Manila trade.

The Manila Galleon. The route of the Manila galleon[8] was paramount not only in the further exploration of the California coast from Cabo San Lucas to the northern California region but in the establishment of permanent sea-lanes between the north and south. Once established, these sea routes helped maintain communication between Baja California, Alta California, and the mainland. These sea-lanes remained permanent migration routes between Baja and Alta California to the present. At the turn of the twentieth century families in the extreme south used these same passages as primary migratory routes between San Diego and Baja California.

The California coast became an immediate concern of the Spanish Crown because of the need for coastal refuges for the Manila galleon on its long voyages. The winds and ocean currents of the Pacific produced natural sea-lanes (the California current) that brought the galleons to the cape, and Cabo San Lucas became a natural resting spot where the ships could readily put in for water and repairs. But additional ports were needed elsewhere along the coast, and new explorations centered around their discovery.

The ensuing years saw several exploratory voyages to the northwest to seek a passage for the Philippine galleons. These included the voyage of Sebastian Rodriguez de Cermeño, who sailed first to the Philippines from Acapulco. Almost simultaneously with Cermeño's return, the viceroy commissioned Sebastian Vizcaíno to explore the Gulf of California and to establish settlements on the peninsula (Bolton 1908:44). On two successive voyages in 1599 Vizcaíno explored the inner gulf coast from La Paz and later Magdalena Bay, Cedros Island, San Diego Bay (which received its name on this voyage), Santa Catalina, and Monterey Bay (Bolton 1908:46–48). But the search for a port on the Pacific coast ended with the voyage of Vizcaíno. He had explored and mapped the Pacific coast thoroughly but had failed to secure a port for the galleon.

Until the late sixteenth century the exploration of the Pacific coast had kept pace with the general Spanish penetration of the continent, but continuing failure to secure good settlements and harbors along the coast and the growing recognition that the peninsula was a marginally productive region combined to shift attention away from the coast and peninsula. The seventeenth century witnessed surging development on the mainland while Baja California stagnated. This peripheral nature of Baja California within the New Spanish system was furthermore compounded by the threat posed by the English buccaneers, Drake, Cavendish, and later Woodes Rogers and George Shelvoke (Englehardt 1929:29–31), who all roamed the open seas plundering Spanish vessels. In addition, Dutch freebooters had established themselves at Pichilingue outside of La Paz and were a constant menace to mainlanders (Engelhardt 1929:80).

The Spanish population of the mainland had settled in the sixteenth century and by 1550 had begun to branch northward to open new lands and eventually new economic bases for the Spanish. Mexico itself was becoming more and more independent of Spain. The clergy, who had entered Mexico during the conquest, made the northern expansion successful. The church made a great investment in evangelization on the mainland, but this interest was not to be seen in Baja California until the next century.

In brief, Baja California provided no riches, no great cities, and no great populations to evangelize. Furthermore, colonists saw Baja as a barren wasteland in which the European could not live. All the settlements attempted between 1533 and 1680 had failed. There was no water, and all provisions had to be imported across a sea plagued by dangerous currents and winds. The only predictability in Baja California was the lack of rain. Expeditions up the Pacific coast in search of suitable harbor and settlement locations brought no immediate benefit to the Spanish. They did place California on the cartographic map of the world and set the stage for communication, future settlement, and mobility in the Californias.

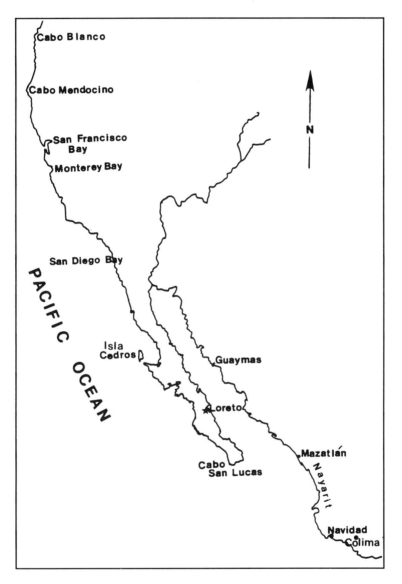

Map 2.
Pacific West Coast of
Alta and Baja California

The Settlement and Colonization of the Peninsula

Not until 1678, over a century after discovery, did the Spanish government make a determined effort to establish a permanent settlement in Baja California. The government made plans, built ships and entrusted the spiritual conquest of California to the Society of Jesus (Engelhardt 1929:83).[9]

The Jesuits, Franciscans, and Dominicans. Fray Eusebio Francisco Kino entered the Baja peninsula in 1683 and became the key figure in the establishment of the Jesuits in Baja California. Kino's expedition went first to La Paz, but because of conflicts with indigenous groups he was forced north to San Bruno. There Kino and his fellow friars established contacts with the natives of the region and began learning their language. San Bruno was a barren outpost and displeased the military contingent, under the command of Admiral Isidro Otondo y Antillon. They decided to abandon the settlement. Kino begged to remain on the peninsula and, when forced to leave, promised the natives he would return. Impressed with the Indians' good nature, Kino committed himself to the establishment of a mission chain in California. He thought the natives were ready for conversion and he visualized future mission sites where native rancherías were located.[10] (Some of these sites became twentieth-century townships from which migrants headed north along the same trails and roads developed in the missionary period.) Although Kino was committed to return to San Bruno, he could find no immediate support in New Spain from either his superiors or the viceregal government. He was assigned to Sonora, where he remained his entire career.

The difficulty of gaining authorization for the peninsula mission chain illustrates the unfavorable disposition of the Mexican religious and political authorities. The government had made successive expenditures in the Californias, had received little in return, and had abandoned any thought of successful economic gain. The peninsula had become a reality of successive failures. There was no gold, no great population, only a barren, inhospitable, and waterless region from which no civilized man could squeeze even his subsistence. The difficult condition of life there secured Baja California's isolation from the mainland even after colonization, settlement, and population of the peninsula had taken place.

Juan María de Salvatierra, the new visitor-general for the Jesuits in Sonora and Sinaloa, met Fray Kino a year after his return from Baja and became empassioned with the concept of developing a mission chain in California. For the next ten years Salvatierra and Kino argued for the mission chain at all levels of religious and governmental administration. But not until 1696 did they find sympathetic ears. The idea of a mission settlement in Baja California was then finally approved (by the superior general of the Jesuits and the audencia), whereupon Salvatierra solicited alms for the project. Fray Kino was forced to stay behind because of an Indian uprising in Sonora. Before Fr. Salvatierra left Fray Francisco María Pícolo was named to replace Kino, but Salvatierra could not wait and left for the peninsula; Pícolo joined him later (Engelhardt 1929:101–102).[11]

Fr. Salvatierra embarked for the peninsula in 1697, accompanied by Captain Luis de Torres y Tortolero, first ensign of the garrison of California, five soldiers, and three mainland Indians (Venegas 1759:227). This small group[12] formed the basis for a successful settlement and for the establishment of a permanent mestizo/criollo populace in the Californias. (Among these individuals was Nicolas Marquez, a Sicilian soldier whose descendant, Loreto Marquez, is a principal figure in the family migration I describe in later chapters.) Father Salvatierra and his group landed at Loreto (named after Nuestra Señora de Loreto), but it took them two years to establish themselves. During these first two years Salvatierra learned the local language and began successful evangelization and conversion. These years were not without their difficulties. Several skirmishes with Indians, confrontations between local groups, and the struggle for subsistence made frontier life on the peninsula a constant threat to survival. All provisions continued to be supplied from the mainland. Regardless of the hardships, by 1700 there were seventy colonists at Loreto, including Spaniards, mestizos, and Christian Indians from Mexico (Engelhardt 1929:105–113).

Loreto became not only the first successful settlement in the Californias but also the capital and hub of peninsular activity. As inland settlements grew, the majority of Spanish and mestizo movements into the interior came from Loreto. The town was the political and religious capital of the Californias and the base of operations for all religious and military expeditions that entered the northern frontera region of the present U.S.-Mexico border.

The second mission site, San Xavier (1699), was vitally important because in addition to expanding the Spanish colonial territory it provided a peninsular source of provisions and firmly rooted the Jesuits on the peninsula. Friar Juan de Ugarte, who had joined Salvatierra and Fray Pícolo (Kino's replacement) on the peninsula, made San Xavier the breadbasket of the colony. There he cultivated the first grapes in the Californias, exported the first California wines to the mainland, bred horses, raised sheep for their wool and wheat for bread. He taught weaving and carpentry and was known to participate in all the work of the mission (Engelhardt 1929; Venegas 1759; Clavigero 1937, 1971).

By 1702 the mission chain was a reality and the Jesuits had managed to secure further support in New Spain. Three missions had been founded: Loreto, San Francisco Xavier, and Nuestra Señora de los Dolores del Sur. Furthermore, rancherías throughout each of the mission areas were visited regularly by the fathers. That same year Fray Pícolo went to Mexico for support of the missions of California. In addition to securing much needed supplies, Pícolo managed to obtain donations for new missions. These missions were to be San José de Comondú, La Purisma Concepción, Our Lady of Guadalupe, and Santa Rosalía de Mulegé.

The Jesuit period came to an abrupt end when the society was expelled from the New World in 1767. But in a seventy-year period the Jesuits had succeeded in establishing fourteen successful mission sites that extended from the cape at San José del Cabo to Santa María de Calamajue at about the thirtieth parallel. Their explorations of the northern area paved the way for the Franciscan entrance into the north and set the stage for the initial settlement of the Californias.

Although the Jesuits succeeded in colonizing the peninsula, the natural environment confined them to specific areas. Geography remained a constant barrier to missionary as well as Spanish colonial. They were forced to use the natural paths and roads used by native Californios in seasonal migrations between springs, water holes, and areas of subsistence gathering. Individual Jesuits founded mission sites within areas of denser native populations and through *visitas* to neighboring and surrounding rancherías the religious chain spread throughout the southern portion of the peninsula. Once established at mission sites, settlers continued to use the natural paths and travel routes between towns and localities.

The Jesuit experience in the peninsula set the pattern of settlement and mobility in the peninsula. Mission sites grew into small but prominent populations of individuals who came to call Baja California Sur their home. The combined effect of the geographic barriers of the peninsula and the isolation from the mainland created strong ties between towns and their populations.

At the time of their expulsion, the Jesuits had reached the boundaries of the frontera region in the north and had established the present route of El Camino Real. It became the main artery to the north as it passed through prominent mission and town sites. In later years news about the north came through the mission spots as travelers moved between the sectors.

Following the Jesuit expulsion the Franciscans (1768) and Dominicans (1773) entered the peninsula, but they turned the emphasis of settlement toward the north. Baja California Sur reverted to its peripheral position as it lost the interest of the missionaries. The move toward the north was the result of growing competition between the Dominican and Franciscan orders as well as the product of the king's desire to control northern Pacific ports. Upon expulsion of the Jesuits the Dominicans had petitioned for their share of California. But the Franciscans had already established themselves in San Diego and Monterey. These ports were vital to the Crown and the government of New Spain required their immediate occupancy. Since the Franciscans had laid claim to the ports, under Fray Junipero Serra they became advocates of the settlement of Alta California. The resulting conflict between the orders resulted in the division of California. Through a concordat in 1772 the Dominicans took charge of the old Jesuit missions, which the Franciscans had allowed to fall into disrepair, and were assigned the frontera region extending from the last northern missions of the peninsula almost to San Diego. The Franciscans took charge of Alta California, including San Diego and the area north. Three Franciscan sites were established north of San Diego in 1772, while the Dominicans extended the peninsular missions north to the frontier.

The Dominican chain facilitated travel and communication between the Californias. Once missionaries had pacified the natives, the frontera became safe for travel to the north. The Dominican-dominated frontera became the northern connection to the southern peninsular towns as well as to New Spain on the mainland. The richer lands in Alta California became the targets of planned settlement, but Baja California remained a way station in the process.

Loreto, however, remained the religious and political capital of the Californias. All supplies, communication, and exploratory expeditions were initiated in Loreto. El Camino Real, as the developed route to the

San Diego

San Miguel
Guadalupe

SONORA

Santo
Tomás · Santa
Catarina

San Vicente

Santo Domingo
· San Pedro
Martir

El Rosario

San
Fernando
·Santa María
·Calamajue

GULF of

N

San
Borja

Santa
·Gertrudis

CALIFORNIA

San
·Ignacio
·Guadalupe

Santa Rosalía
de Mulegé

PACIFIC

La Purísima
Concepción ·

·San Bruno
·San José de Comondú
·Nuestra Señora
de Loreto

San Francisco
Xavier ·

Nuestra Señora
de Dolores·

MISSION
DEVELOPMENT

San Luis
Gonzaga

El Pilar de
La Paz

	Jesuit
	Franciscan
	Dominican

Todos
Santos

Santiago

San José
del
Cabo

(from Meigs 1935: vi)

Map 3.

north, kept the peninsula within the active northward expansion. Lines of communication were kept open for continuing expeditions as well as for later movement between the peninsula and Alta California.

The historical and geographic settlement processes that contributed to a regional pattern of mobility in Baja and Alta California were initiated by the Spanish in their explorations along the Pacific coast in the sixteenth and seventeenth centuries. The progress of the missionaries from south to north and their ultimate emphasis on the frontera region and Alta California strengthened the northern orientation of these patterns. As a result, the peninsular population was continually oriented northward. The region from Monterey to the cape became a Spanish-dominated sociocultural domain in which the towns of the peninsula became points in a matrix of mobility and communication which lasted until the twentieth century.

– 2 –

NINETEENTH-CENTURY DEVELOPMENTS: THE SOCIOECONOMIC CONTEXT OF MIGRATION

At the beginning of the nineteenth century communication and relations between the two Californias were well established. Alta and Baja California shared a regionally specific history that set the basis for identifying the Californias as a distinct sociocultural area. Mobility between the towns of the southern peninsula and Alta California was relatively frequent, although Baja continued to be preceived by the mainlanders and others as the way station to the north. The government saw Alta California as the greener pasture. What Baja lacked could be found in abundance in the north. Rain, a more temperate climate, safe ports, and good settlement sites were common in Alta California, whereas in Baja such attributes were rare gems. The pattern of California communication and interrelations intensified in the nineteenth century. The foreign development of whaling, otter hunting, and mining affected the peninsula as nothing else had in previous postcontact history.

FOREIGN INTERESTS
AND THE DEVELOPMENT OF MINING

At the close of the eighteenth century Alta California remained the focus of Spanish attention as Baja California stagnated. "The northern limits of the Dominican frontier had been reached, the Indians resisted further proselytizing, and the attention of the Spanish government was turned to the more fertile fields of Alta California" (Meadows 1915:15).

The separation of upper and lower California in 1804 added to Baja's continuing neglect by the Spanish mainland government. This general disregard contributed greatly to the rise of foreign interests in the peninsula. During the early nineteenth century a surge of foreigners entered the peninsula, setting a pattern that would continue through the entire century. These foreign interests in Baja can be analyzed within the framework of Mexican history and Mexican national development policy in the nineteenth century and can be understood within the historical pattern of Baja California's ties with the north.

The Baja Coast: Open Territory

In the early 1800s the discovery of rich sea otter colonies along the west coast of the Baja peninsula first attracted American and English hunters and traders, who were later joined by Russians and even occasional Aleuts (Bancroft 1889:707). A trade network between missions, peninsular inhabitants, and foreigners developed and began to prosper in the next half century. Despite Spanish demands to end this trade with foreigners, commerce grew and a primary base for American vessels was established at San Quintín. This marked the beginnings of American and English footholds in Baja. Later, when the Mexican national government took over, the sea otter trade expanded south to Magdalena Bay, some eight hundred miles south of the present international border.

The Revival of Mining

Mining had been a principal interest in the Mexican economy from the time of the conquest, but its revival in the nineteenth century took impetus from the needs of the developing Mexican nation. After the War of Independence (1810–1821) Mexican interests in foreign involvement in Mexican mining slowly built up. Independence had caused great upheaval throughout Mexico, and mines, mining towns, mints, and Spanish workings had been destroyed. Attempting to stabilize the economy and bring in needed capital, Mexico adopted a more liberal attitude toward foreigners after the war. Mining began to recover, and in 1823 legal prohibitions against foreigners' owning mines in Mexico were relaxed. First the British, stirred by fantastic stories of rich Mexican ores, invested and began developing mining areas. But by the 1840s British firms on the mainland were on the downswing. In contrast, the peninsula otter trade was prospering, and a new source of foreign exploitation was beginning. The discovery of the breeding grounds of the grey whale on the mid-peninsula provided an easy and profitable resource for American and British whalers. Small mines that had been granted as concessions to English firms on the peninsula petered out, but the otter and whaling activity increased and fostered small settlements along the coast.[1]

In a further effort to maintain and stimulate foreign capital in Mexico the government eased the remaining barriers to foreign investment and offered rewards for the discovery of ores and mercury. In the last decade of the forties, the production of precious metals increased slightly, but Mexico (and Baja California) was soon to experience a series of crises that discouraged foreign investment.

Baja and the U.S.-Mexican War

The War of 1846–1848 with the U.S. aroused the patriotic sentiments of Baja Californios as no other conflict in Mexican history. The U.S. occupied Baja California from 1847 to 1848 and repelled a series of attacks from small groups of patriotic forces in the cape region.[2] Ironically, however, the war also prompted emigration to the United States by numerous individuals who favored U.S. rule (see Martinez 1965; North 1908). Moreover, the neutral stance taken by the governor of Baja California when the war broke out furnished another sign of the region's northward orientation. In the end the war and its effects in Baja California served to legitimize the peninsula as Mexican, both because of the national sentiment aroused in the populace (those who stayed) and because of the terms of the treaty of Guadalupe Hidalgo. Although the U.S. had occupied Baja and there was great pressure in Alta California to include the peninsula as a U.S. territory, Mexico retained the peninsula and a narrow strip of land in the north that would assure its geographic connection to the mainland. Mexico's humiliation at losing half of her territory was enough; loss of the peninsula would have been salt in the wound.[3] The mixed reactions of the peninsular people during the war illustrate the ties between the Californias. Such sentiments, based on historic patterns of personal relations, were to be long-lasting and would again be expressed in the northward movement, and settlement of peninsulars in the twentieth century.

The "loss" of Baja California was scornfully accepted by U.S. citizens, especially those who had vested interests there. So disgruntled were some that during the remaining half century a number of private adventurers attempted to conquer the peninsula through an action known as "filibustering." Based in San Francisco, the filibusters launched attacks on Baja California and Sonora. Among the most prominent of these adventurers were Charles de Pindray, Raousset-Boulbon, Joseph Morehead, and William Walker.[4] These rogues were viewed as heroes in California as they marched south in blatant illegal acts against Mexico (Blaisdell 1962; Bancroft 1889; Martinez 1960; Jordan 1951).

The California Gold Rush: Baja Rediscovered

By mid-century another event took place that not only increased foreign involvement in Baja California but changed the northwestern coast of America: the California gold rush. The repercussions of the California gold strike were worldwide. In Baja and the Mexican mainland the boom meant incorporation into a world economy. The migration of Baja Californios and the family networks in the mining towns and along the border thus became not just local, isolated events but responses in a long chain of historic events intimately tied to developments on the continental and world level. The decision of individuals and families to migrate can be better understood within these contexts.

During the mid-nineteenth century the entire world experienced rapid socioeconomic change, marked by the rise of capitalist enterprise and the true beginnings of industrialization. Until this time Baja California had been only a peripheral element in the Mexican and Spanish role in the world economy. Baja's main asset was its geographic position, which served as a stepping-stone first to (and from) the Philippines and later to the north. The gold rush marked the beginnings of a new onslaught on foreign investment and development on Mexico's west coast.

The California gold strike, in a remote area of a virtually unpopulated sector of the world, reopened the channels of communication and transport along the entire west coast of the American continent. The old Spanish lanes of commerce, developed during the heyday of the Manila galleon, were given new life as people migrated to California from all parts of the world. The gold fever spread across the oceans and began to draw people from Central and South America, Asia, and Europe. The immigrant trade brought an increase in shipping and created new networks of transport that incorporated the western coast of America into the world market. Increased immigration from Europe brought more ships around the cape and influenced the development of the only railroad across the isthmus of Panama. Tehuantepec, as well as Panama, became bustling avenues of trade that facilitated Chilean, Mexican, Asian, and U.S. trade with Europe (see Hobsbawm 1975: esp. 61–65).

For Baja California the gold rush meant rediscovery. Ships carried immigrants to the peninsula and communication between Alta and Baja intensified. During this period many ancestors of twentieth-century migrants to the U.S. arrived in the peninsula, and many cape families traveled between Alta and Baja California. Furthermore, a new wave of Americans began moving south at this time.

The cape towns were first exposed to a variety of travelers en route north to Alta California. Gold seekers who were unable to get transport directly to San Francisco (from Panama) chartered small vessels and went up the coast to San Blas or Mazatlán traveling from there to La Paz.

> ... They [then] turned inland following the paths of the padres northward along the El Camino Real. . . . All of them left a record of hardiness still fresh in the memory of the old Mexicans who refer to their route as the camino to the California placers. Invariably these pioneers traveled from La Paz to Dolores del Sur, thence northwesterly to Jesus María, San Xavier, Comondú, Purisima, San Ignacio, Ojo de Liebre, San Andreas, Rosario, and then up the line of coast missions. (North 1908:70)

The movement of individuals through the peninsula affected later travel north as well as the composition of the towns themselves. Individuals who were attracted to the life on the southern peninsula often settled, others returned after the gold rush, and some peninsulars themselves made their first personal contacts with the region to the north.

Americans showed great interest in the peninsula as part of the geographic extension of Alta California. They believed that Baja would yield mineral strikes similar to those of Alta California. Lured by stories of rich mineral veins and an occasional strike, desert prospectors, company mineralogists, and lone gold seekers began entering the peninsula in the mid-eighteenth century.

After the War of the Reform (1857–1861), political leaders seeking to stabilize Mexico's economy sought increased foreign involvement, including that from the U.S. Mexico had struggled through a period of reorganization, and the greed and corruption of General Santa Anna had finally provoked war.[5] Attempting to bring internal stability, Benito Juárez inaugurated a new constitution (1857) that institutionalized a laissez-faire policy opening the door for foreign involvement. Faced with a collapsing economy, Mexican national policy sought the capital of foreigners to help develop a stable economy with which to back political reforms. For Juárez and his government, the answer was to develop and settle Baja and other Mexican outposts.

The intervention of the French (1861–1867) caused internal conflict and setbacks for the Mexican republic, but Baja California was isolated enough to remain outside the French grasp in Mexico (Martinez 1960). The northern peninsula, like the west coast isolated and virtually unpopulated, emerged relatively unscathed from these bouts. The French presence did not limit the activity of the foreign interests in the north.

THE PORFIRIATO: FOREIGN CONCESSIONS AND THE MINING ECONOMY, 1870–1900

The policies of Porfirio Díaz, president of Mexico from 1877 to 1911, crystallized the laissez-faire trends begun by Benito Juárez. During the period of the Porfiriato (1877–1911), in Baja, as throughout Mexico, the government encouraged foreign investment as its principal development policy. In addition to the problem of capital, Mexico also lacked the technical knowledge to promote the development and production of her economy. Díaz, who favored the development of the nation by the economically powerful, encouraged foreign investment through legal statutes that leaned heavily in favor of foreigners.[6] As a result, American, British, and French capitalists competed for control of Mexico's resources.

American Investments

Although foreign investments of all types were eventually encouraged by the Díaz regime, the American investor played the dominant role in the rapid economic development of the period.[7] Mexico's new policies of economic liberty seemed to be aimed at the competitive American businessman. By 1885 an estimated forty American firms were working in Mexico (Bernstein 1964:19).

American business soon made extensive investments in Baja California. The peninsula, with its historic ties to the north and its isolation from the mainland, was an inviting, often irresistible, frontier for U.S. economic adventures. In 1864 the Juárez government made the first large land grant in Baja California to the Lower California Colonization and Mining Company. This grant included nearly 47,000 square miles, for which the company was to pay $100,000.[8]

The most famous of the Díaz schemes involved the International Company. In 1884 Díaz granted a charter for the entire northern half of the peninsula to the International Company of Mexico, an American company headquartered in Hartford, Connecticut. The grant contained some 18 million acres (28,000 square miles). (It was resold in 1889 to the Mexican Land and Colonization Company, an English corporation.) That same year, Flores, Hale, and Company was granted a tract that included about 4 million acres (the tract was later brought under the direction of the Chartered Company of Lower California, a Boston-New York syndicate). The following year a French company took over the interests of Moeller and Company, a German business operating out of Guaymas, and obtained a liberal concession covering over 50,000 acres. This concession, to be known as El Boleo, became the most successful in the entire peninsula.

Foreign Antecedents of Baja Californios

The influx of foreigners into Mexico had greater effects on the demographic composition of Baja California than on other parts of the republic. The peninsula's historic ties with the north were not only intensified but now peninsulars and foreigners interacted across class and within class levels. Native peninsulars had had early contact with a host of Europeans during the years of illegal otter trade and later during the era of coastal whaling. Settlements along the west coast (San Quintín and Magdalena Bay) brought peninsulars and Europeans face to face. During the mid-nineteenth century numerous sailors and businessmen married and settled in the cape region. Towns such as Comondú, Loreto, and Mulegé were especially affected, and the family names of Drew, McLish, Smith, McIntosh, Simpson, and Green, now part of Baja lore, appeared at this time. Given the numerous foreign inroads in the peninsula, it is no wonder that mestizo families migrating north across the border at the turn of the century consisted of descendants of English (Smiths), Peruvian (Castellanos), German (Bolume), Irish (Simpson), Sicilian (Marquez), and other foreigners who had been incorporated into the existing population and had made the peninsula their home.

The Technological Development of Mining

Mining during the Porfiriato and throughout the world in the late nineteenth century experienced rapid technological development. Prior to the mid-nineteenth century, great quantities of silver and gold had been extracted from Mexico under Spanish rule. Although technologically advanced for their time, the Spanish virtually raped ore deposits. They extracted ore without concern for human lives or geographic locales. After the War of Independence, English steam engines, pumps, and techniques were introduced into Mexico, but the techniques were costly and the effort proved a failure. After the U.S.-Mexican war, Mexican mining made fast progress. The political posture in Mexico, the laissez-faire policy, the spread of capitalist interests and parallel developments in mining technology promoted the extraction of Mexican ores. A shift from silver mining to emphasis on nonferrous metals, iron, coal, and oil necessitated modern techniques and encouraged technological advance in almost all arenas associated with mining. When Americans entered Mexico after mid-century, they introduced the techniques of stamp-milling, panamalgamation of silver ore, and blast furnace smelters. The result was the opening of a series of new districts.

Although new machinery and techniques reinvigorated the Mexican mining industry, the prominent flow of natural resources continued going out of Mexico. Shipments of high-grade ore to Europe from regions as remote as Oaxaca, Sonora, and Baja California were common. Smelters located in foreign countries relied on the Mexican mines (see Bernstein 1964, chapters 2, 3, and 4).

Progress of Transportation

Increasing production and extraction of ores in both old and new districts stimulated improvements in Mexico's outdated transport system. On the mainland American investors built roads into new areas, opening untapped districts. The need to get into newly discovered districts and transport raw materials from outpost sites and throughout Mexico were major factors in the development of Mexico's railroad system in the late 1880s.[9] The earliest railroad lines fed directly in and out of the mainland mining districts of the north and linked up with U.S. lines. Between 1883 and 1885 the north had a direct outlet to American smelters in Colorado, Kansas, Missouri, and Oklahoma.[10] Further developments in transport (extensions of the railroad system), support industries, and technology in Mexico came only after the U.S. stiffened import controls. In 1890 the McKinley Tariff Act imposed controls on incoming ores, causing a shift of American interests within Mexico. Thereafter, American investors built smelters in Mexico, expanded the rail system, and developed coal mining in order to provide the essential power for railroads and smelters. Not only did the mining districts become more independent but bulk exports became economically feasible.

Except for the El Boleo concession, mining developments in the peninsula never gained the prominence of those on the mainland. Baja mines remained isolated and added only peripherally to the economic development of the region, hindered by a lack of roads, small population centers (for labor), and extreme aridity. Furthermore, most if not all the mining exploits were short-term. As in the colonial and missionary periods, Baja's main barrier to settlement and development continued to be physical geography. The ore strikes, although numerous, were short-lived, and districts that attracted hundreds and occasionally thousands of prospectors were quickly abandoned. The Baja mines never reached the maturity so often associated with frontier boomtowns in the rest of the west. The peninsula mines generally produced no lasting settlements. Once the ore was exhausted, the prospectors, laborers, and company moved out, taking everything they owned. They disassembled machinery, transported it to the coast, loaded it on dinghies, and shipped it back to Alta California or to a new boom area.

Throughout the last half of the nineteenth century peninsula travelers continued to rely on the old mission trails that followed natural geographical passages. On the mainland railroads had opened districts and provided the primary transport for the export of ore and the import of necessary goods and supplies. But Baja would not have a major railroad until 1948.[11] As in the seventeenth and eighteenth centuries, the waters of the Pacific and the gulf provided access to the entire peninsula and made the transport of machinery to isolated districts possible. Mules and wagons to carry new machines, lumber, foodstuffs, and people were all shipped in. When the boom fizzled, the equipment was again shipped out.

Steam travel between Baja and Alta California had been revived during the '49 gold rush and increased tremendously at the turn of the century. The International Company, like other large concessions, began periodic steam shipments between various towns along the Pacific and gulf. Travel between San Francisco, San Diego, Ensenada, Magdalena Bay, La Paz, and mainland ports became regular.

The Baja Mining Circuit and Peninsular Families

While most mines on the mainland were worked by an ample local labor pool, Baja California first depended on imported labor. Around mid-century groups of Yaquis were brought across the gulf to work the new mines. Only later did peninsulars begin heading to the interior mines (see Aschmann 1967; Bernstein 1964; Martinez 1965; North 1908). The mines were supported by migrant populations that soon were making the labor circuit of the mines much like the great *piscas* (seasonal fruit-picking migrations) of Alta California in the twentieth century.

During this short period mining became a way of life for the individuals who moved up and down the Baja peninsula from mine to mine. The baja *barretero* (miner) viewed his existence as dependent on mining in the peninsula. The mines, mining towns, and their geography became a principal aspect of family lore.

Peninsular miners worked and traveled to various spots on the mainland as well (see chapter 5). During the late 1880s and particularly in the early twentieth century the copper mines of Cananea attracted numerous peninsular families. Many of these individuals worked in Santa Rosalía and learned valuable skills that they transferred to other jobs during their lives.

The peninsular miners and families of this study came primarily from the southern portion of the peninsula. The small rancho towns there were unable to support growing populations and the mines provided an outlet. In the late 1880s and early 1890s the mines of San Juan (in Las Flores on the Gulf Coast) and Calmallí in the central desert attracted individuals and families from the cape region and from the mainland west coast. Many families traveled to join relatives with hopes

Typical gold and silver mine in Mexico showing methods of interior mining, *barreteros* (miners), peons, and the gang leader (*capataz*). September 1890. (Bain Collection, Library of Congress)

of participating in the mining ventures. Later, in the late 1890s, families migrated into the northern peninsula mines of Punta Prieta, Julio César, El Marmol, and El Alamo.

The peninsular families, unlike the miners of the gold strikes of Alta California, became company miners. The large placers required shaft operations and smelter work in which semiskilled labor could be used. The majority of these migrants were not aiming to strike it rich but were seeking employment and a life-style similar to what they knew in their hometowns in the south. They became *barreteros*, miners who actually worked within the mines or shafts, and a few subsisted on the support economies of such as *leñadores* (wood collectors) and small store operators. These individuals formed the working class component of the mine operations, under the supervision of the company engineers and managers.

The social interaction between the English, American, and French company men and peninsulars was very different from that in previous decades of foreign immigration. Where peninsulars had intermarried and interacted socially with the otter traders, whalers, and others during the early mid-century, the mines produced a labor-company stratification. Company managers and operators separated themselves socially from the common mine laborers and their families.

Although the mines of Baja California were quickly exhausted and abandoned by capitalists, these mines stimulated development of the border region in Alta California. Small economies in San Diego blossomed and expanded because of the mining boom in Baja. The port of San Diego bustled with steamers heading to the south loaded with passengers, materials, and foodstuffs. Furthermore, populations of San Diego and Southern California, having increased tremendously during the land boom of the late 1800s, became increasingly aware of available land on the peninsula. Developments along the U.S. side of the border began entering the adjacent border lands and were to bring land and population development of the frontera region as a whole. The Porfiriato foreign investment policies that had brought about the development of mining also stimulated the development of the frontera.

THE DEVELOPMENT OF THE FRONTERA

In the early twentieth century the entire border began to change from a quiet, unpopulated region to a region of urban centers. Immigrants entered the area in increasing numbers and the towns of the border entered a growth phase that would characterize the region for the next seventy-five years. Although the Imperial Valley of California and Mexicali valley had not developed and the 1920s influx of mainland Mexicanos had not yet begun, the city of San Diego was growing fast and the cotton boom soon pushed Mexicali into the wider continental picture.

The West Coast of North America contributed to the growth of intensive capitalism in the world economic system in the late nineteenth century and the early decades of the twentieth. The foreign capital investments of the Porfiriato, first in mining, then in the region of the border, not only stimulated the growth of towns but also fit the general pattern of a new moralistic and materialistic cycle that became the major western world economic philosophy in the twentieth century. In the towns of Tijuana and Mexicali American investments controlled and directed the profile of growth and development.

American land investment interests in the Mexicali region procured the extension of the Imperial Valley canal system that would foster the development of that valley and bring water into Mexicali. Water was the single requirement for turning the region into a world cotton production region. Lands controlled by the American Land and Cattle Company were leased and soon producing vast quantities of cotton, which required labor for primary production, cultivation, and harvesting as well as for supporting industries.

Calexico, in the U.S., was the first center of the Mexicali valley, American businesses, investment firms, and banks began to direct their efforts toward the Mexicali valley. As the population center of the northern gulf, Calexico attracted early settlers from the mining circuit and from the cape region of the peninsula. Calexico continued growing but by the early 1920s it was surpassed by Mexicali, which became the Gulf Coast center of economic trade and travel.

Ensenada, on the west coast, had become the capital city of the north primarily because of the investments of the International Company (the Connecticut-based corporation whose concession of sixteen million acres was later transferred to a British firm). At the turn of the century the city was the major center of trade and population as well as the primary port of steam travel from San Diego for American and English interests in the northern peninsula. San Quintín, about 120 miles south, and various coastal outlets for interior mines relied on communication and shipments from Ensenada and San Diego.

Tijuana grew from a small rancho in the 1800s to a sizable town in the early twentieth century, primarily as a result of increasing traffic across the border. In the mid-nineteenth century Tijuana was a collective of private ranchos, and toward the end of the century the only government presence in the area was a border station set up to tax traffic to Ensenada. Traffic south across the border increased tremendously during the Santa Clara gold strike in 1889 when thousands of gold-hungry Americans crossed the line. "The rush of argonauts passing through San Diego from late February to mid-March (1889) averaged about 300 a day. On March 5th, near the peak of the fever, 600 left San Diego for the mines—over 100 by steamer and the rest by train, wagon, burro, or foot toward Tijuana" (Lingenfelter 1967:12). One observer wrote: "Every person seemed to have some portion of the excitement about him, and the most common question in the street was, 'When are you going to leave?'" (Ibid.:5).

Tijuana's growth into the great metropolitan city of today began in its attraction for tourists from the nearby and growing city of San Diego. Tourism, centered around American capital interests in gambling, horse racing, and cabarets, began prior to the First World War, but the dramatic upswing in investment and development in Tijuana came in the 1920s with the advent of prohibition in the United States. During the twenties Tijuana and Ensenada were havens for American pleasure-seekers. Famous for plush gambling casinos, hotels, and cabarets, Tijuana became a crossroad, and place of entrance, to and from San Diego. Meanwhile, another part of Tijuana unknown to the tourist was developing. The Mexican government built roads along the border, and labor for Tijuana's tourist industry necessitated the establishment of regular Mexican institutions. Government and private sectors established markets, housing, parks, churches, and social services of all types for the Mexican population. Tijuana was soon established as a regular Mexican town, but Americans knew only the tourist attractions.

Population changes in the frontera towns are especially illustrative of the area's growth. In 1910 and 1920 the Mexican census classified Tijuana as one of the pueblos in the greater *municipalidad* of Ensenada.[12] In 1920 Tijuana had a population of 1,928, which placed it in the *pueblo* classification. Ensenada (with 2,178 inhabitants) and Mexicali (with 6,782) had populations greater than 2,000 and were classed by the census of 1921 as the only cities of the north (Censo General de la Nacion: 1921). During the same basic period the city of Mexicali grew from a total of 462 inhabitants in 1910 to 6,782 in 1920, when there were almost 15,000 people in the entire township. These figures were to change dramatically in the next few decades.

At the end of the twenties when the second stream of Baja families was moving north, Tijuana was becoming established as a major Mexican crossing point and settlement area. By 1930 Tijuana had grown from a pueblo of less than 2,000 people to a township of 11,271; within three decades it would surpass 165,000. Mexicali similarly experienced phenomenal growth and in 1930 reached 29,985. Ensenada, with 7,000, was still growing but would continue to be surpassed by the northern cities.

Across the border a parallel development prevailed. San Diego continued the geometric growth begun during the land boom of the 1880s (McWilliams 1973:113–137). The city's 1910 population of 39,578 almost doubled in the next decade to 74,361 and by 1930 it was 147,995 (U.S. Census, 1930). In addition, the nineteenth-century developments on the peninsula greatly affected San Diego as a principal port and commercial city. Shipping along the coast had increased first with the otter and seal trade along the western peninsula. The forty-niner gold rush added tremendously to this traffic. As various companies established mines in the south, San Diego became the major port of call for company steamers. Traffic to the south continued to grow, and travel to various peninsular ports became regular. San Diego profited from the need to import practically all foodstuffs, lumber, machinery, and living supplies to the southern company mines in Baja. Although the city's commercial strength grew throughout the mid- and late nineteenth century, the most intense benefit came in the late 1880s. Miners and merchants of all types were attracted to San Diego, and as early as 1870 San Diego merchants bought the majority of gold coming out of the small but rich gold strikes in the northern peninsula (Stern 1973:28). Between 1870 and the turn of the century travelers headed to the mines of the south passed through San Diego and procured their supplies there. The editor of the *San Diego Bee* of 1885 described the benefits clearly: "It is safe to estimate that fully 5,000 people will go out to the mines, passing through San Diego. These will each spend, at the lowest estimate, an average of $50 per outfit. This means in cold coin a quarter of a million put in circulation here at once" (Lingenfelter 1967:7).

Not only was local commerce prospering but San Diego merchandisers and grocers had branch outlets in the more prosperous mining communities. San Diego businessmen lobbied in Washington first to open free trade between the two regions and then for a new transcontinental railroad (1886) that would pass along the border to San Diego with southern spurs into the mine and cattle-raising districts (Shipek 1965:12).

San Diego was also experiencing the influx of thousands of individuals interested in the land boom in Southern California. The company concessions in Baja, granted by Díaz, attempted to capitalize on this wealth of prospective colonizers and initiated a tremendous campaign to attract settlers to the vast territory to the south. Advertisements appeared daily in the Los Angeles and San Diego newspapers, spelling out the golden opportunities awaiting those fortunate enough to head south (see Lingenfelter 1967; Shipek 1965; Martinez 1965; North 1908).[13] The land boom of Southern California combined with the coastal and mining developments throughout the northern peninsula to spur the growth of this border city.

Although the frontera saw development and change, the peninsular migrant also found continuity in the region. Like the Spanish borderlands, the area from San Diego south to the last Jesuit missions had long been a geographic frontier, the last area the Spanish and Mexicans brought under control. But for the incoming migrant the frontera offered cultural and regional continuity. People spoke Spanish throughout the region; towns had Spanish names and historical backgrounds. Furthermore, communication between the frontera and the south had been continuous. Colonizers, gold seekers, farmers, and cattle raisers from the U.S. traveled south; individuals and families from the south headed north into the growing towns of Southern California. It is in this frontier environment that the pioneer migrants of this study found themselves at the turn of the century. Moving first through the mining circuit during the boom era of the peninsula and then into the border, in its time of rapid development, migrants established social ties and relationships that would form the basis for adaptation within the new socioeconomic environment of the border region and the United States.

-3-

THE SOCIAL, GEOGRAPHIC, AND TEMPORAL BASIS OF NETWORK FORMATION

Many migrant families from the cape region entered Alta California in the late nineteenth and early twentieth centuries. This was the era of Porfiriato economics and border town development that attracted peninsulars and other migrants to the north. Peninsulars migrated to take advantage of economic opportunities, but their moves were facilitated by their regional kinship based on shared experiences. Migrants who settled along the border formalized these relations into a large network of peninsular families. The network was composed first of migrant families that had meandered along the old colonial and mission trails to the boomtowns during the mining period and finally settled along the developing frontera of Alta and Baja California. Afterward, family and friends from the south provided a continuing source for network expansion. The development of this network in three major phases provided the basis for the migrants' adaption and resettlement in the new environment.

Social relations expanded as the network grew in size and incorporated new individuals. The strength of these social ties increased gradually from one phase to the next. Migrants themselves identified and differentiated these periods and spoke of them not only as romanticized reminiscences of "the good old days" but as recognized periods characterized by specific friendships and relations of the past and present.

I have named each phase after a geographic region and characterized each by specific socioeconomic variables that influenced the development of the network. The first phase is called the Calmallí phase for this town acted as a pivotal point in the development of the network. Individual migrants often identify Calmallí as the place where friendships were solidified. This phase includes the initial move from hometowns in the cape region and the meandering northward through the mining towns of the central and northern peninsula. The San Diego-Calexico phase spanned the first two decades of the twentieth century when pioneer migrants crossed the international border and began to settle in the San Diego region. This was a period of initial network formalization in which marriages and *compadrazgo* (godparent) relations were extended between families from the south and the mining circuit. A second stream of migrants from the south during the middle and late 1920s then provided new impetus for establishing family ties and a migrant community in the San Diego-Calexico region. This renewed stream of migrants is also included in the second phase. The third phase took place primarily in the town of Lemon Grove during the thirties and forties and is thus named for that town. During these years a renaissance of community and familial relationships contributed to the formalization of a Baja Californio network in the San Diego region.

The network of families I am describing is characterized by intergenerational membership, continued ties with the peninsula, and a high density of close social relations. The network is primarily composed of a set of families that maintained relations over a period of six generations. At the onset, when people were leaving hometowns, single family units formed the basis for later network development. The actual numbers of this out-migration may never be known, but it was composed of young couples often accompanied by their newly born offspring and older family members. Throughout the phases of migration and development the network remained cross-generational. Grandparents, parents, and offspring of single extended families were always included in the relations between families. On the border the network at its height consisted of at least thirty-five families from both the peninsula and the mainland. Of these I have positively identified eight that passed through Calmallí and had already begun to extend formal family ties. There is inconclusive evidence that at least twice that many families were extending ties. Communication and contact with the towns and people of the south continued throughout the migration process. As families moved north they kept home folk informed about family problems and accomplishments and they received news about hometown family and friends. Participation in hometown networks was kept alive at first through letters and later through visits. Hometown friends and family traveled north to visit, and once migrants had settled along the border they received visitors there and made return visits to the south. Throughout the first phase interactions included most social and family relations. In San Diego Mexican as well as U.S. celebrations, picnics, and dances, in addition to family baptisms, marriages, and funerals, became network events. This network density also came from families' having lived side by side, not only in the neighborhoods of the border but also in the mining towns and the hometowns of the south.

CALMALLÍ: THE MINING CIRCUIT AND EARLY FORMULATION, 1880–1910

Migrants to Calmallí in the late nineteenth and early twentieth century typify families that left hometowns in the south to work in the mines of central and northern Baja California. Families and individuals from various parts of the cape region became acquainted and formed lasting friendships that were solidified by marriage and *compadrazgo*[1] ties. Because travel on the peninsula was limited to horseback, mule, and foot traffic, even direct migration between nearby towns took days and often longer before destinations were reached, particularly when families traveled with children and belongings. Slow but direct routes linked these mining towns, where the basis of community and social ties was established among families who would later seek out and formalize these relationships in the border region.

The initial move from the hometown area was generally motivated by economic and family constraints. Newly married individuals, plus relatives in some cases, were tempted to join sisters, brothers, and other kin in central Baja and farther north. Letters and travelers reported gold strikes, a great inducement to out-migration. But however great the economic possibilities, the move was spurred by the presence of family in the new towns. Not only did family offer security, but a unity of hometown affiliation and a recognized kinship among migrants from a variety of southern pueblos prevailed that was to keep individuals and married couples in close contact throughout the next half century even though circumstances might separate them. Some families settled in northern peninsular towns, while others crossed the international border, moving between the small towns on both sides of the border. This first phase of migration encompassed a large geographic area. Once in the mining towns workers and their families lived side by side and shared everyday experiences. Many young couples began their families in Las Flores and Calmallí, where they raised many of their children. The mines in Baja, however, were not as long-lasting as the families. Each major mine went through boom and bust cycles. When a town lost the ability to support its population, there was generally a boom in another area.

One such area was the Las Flores-Calmallí region. When a mine lost productivity families packed their belongings and made their way to the next mine that could provide jobs. The move from Las Flores to Calmallí is the earliest that includes the families of this study. This move, like others that followed, differed from the initial move from the hometown, when families predominated, and sometimes even families with couples in two generations. The families who moved from Las Flores to Calmallí also included friends whose ties had formed from common residence and experiences in the mines of Las Flores. Individuals knew and were often accompanied by other families who were also moving to the new mines. Once in Calmallí, friendships that had formed in Las Flores and other towns were further solidified. The length of stay in the towns varied, but in Calmallí some families remained as long as ten years. When Calmallí could no longer support the miners, they moved on to the various placer mines of the north. Many would reunite immediately in towns such as Punta Prieta, El Marmol, Julio César, and El Alamo; others would be reunited later in the United States.

CALEXICO AND SAN DIEGO: LA FRONTERA AND EARLY FORMALIZATION, 1910–1930

The second phase of migration can be viewed simply as a continuation of the Calmallí mining phase, which was based both on economic and family motives. But the San Diego-Calexico phase is distinct because of the new sociocultural conditions that developed along the border. Most families initiated this move because of the talk of good jobs and because of the presence of friends and family in specific towns across the border. But the move was different because it involved crossing the international border. Relations intensified because of the new sociocultural conditions. Migrants extended multiple kin ties between families in the form of marriages and *compadrazgo*. These kin ties became the basis for what I call the formalization of the network and they provided a base for cultural and regional identity. When border settlers received a second stream of peninsular migrants, the newcomers added members to the network and increased its kin and friendship basis by reuniting family members and friends. Some families meandered slowly through the small towns of the north into the Mexicali-Calexico region. Others moved directly to San Diego, and many of these eventually headed east into the growing sector of Calexico and Mexicali.

In 1910 Mexicali, with a total population of 462, was only a region of ranches, but Calexico, across the line, was a center of activity for the Mexicali valley. The township of Calexico had a population of 1,887 and the "city" 797. On the west coast Tijuana, which today boasts over a half million inhabitants, was but a private rancho with 273 individuals. The entire northern sector of the peninsula (from Calmallí north to the border) had only 9,760 inhabitants according to the national census, whereas San Diego was a growing metropolis of almost 40,000.

The town of Calexico played a significant role in the formation of the network because it was the principal place where migrants congregated immediately after crossing the border. Although this move followed the pattern of mobility, migrants recognized the crossing of the international border as a move out of Mexico and into the United States. Although many Baja Californios had known and worked with or for Americans in the northern mines, and although various similarities between Alta and Baja California did exist, migrants nonetheless found themselves in a new sociocultural environment that stimulated individuals and families to reestablish ties formed along the northward route to the border. Mutual aid and assistance became a principal part of the pattern as immigrants looked for housing and employment. Many, if not most, initial adjustments to the towns of the United States were made in shared households. As new settlers arrived, they lived with prior migrants who were already established. Employment was often procured with earlier immigrants or through their assistance. Once settled, new families settled close to earlier immigrants.

Social and familial relations were soon strengthened. The old friends of the south pulled together in firm relationships based on the mutual experiences of their northward march, settlement within this new environment, and the extension of aid and assistance offered to both family members and friends in a nondiscriminatory manner. The common tie of regional identity and the extended period of contact through the mining circuit were natural inducements to forming new communities and initiating formal family extensions through marriage and *compadrazgo* ties.

Marriages between pioneer migrants in the 1910–1920 period, although few, served to extend families. Migrant parents generally chose other Baja Californios as godparents for their offspring, thus forming further formal familial extensions through *compadrazgo* relations. The result was the solidification of the social network of friends and families into a formally recognized network of *parientes* (kin). The Calexico phase of network development thus became a base for future extension and solidification.

The Second Stream

The second stream of immigrants increased not only numbers but momentum in network solidification. Regional and family ties were invigorated through this new migration of people. Pioneer migrants into the United States had come at a time when restrictions along the border were virtually nonexistent. Individuals from both the U.S. and the peninsula crossed back and forth with relative ease. This mobility along the frontera continued as the second stream of peninsular families entered the border region. The development of the Mexicali and Imperial valleys encouraged large numbers of mainland immigrants to cross the international border. The second stream of Baja migrants participated in this larger wave, but they came to the border seeking family as well as jobs.

Although the peninsulars of the second stream were aware of the new economic opportunities, the relative success of family and friends in the north reassured their move. These second-stream individuals arrived directly from the hometown regions. Knowledge of sisters, brothers, and other family—this time in Mexicali and San Diego—attracted individuals from Santa Rosalía, Loreto, La Paz, and other Gulf Coast and interior towns. The news of the cotton boom, improved gulf travel, labor contracts, and the security of existing *familia* in the border region combined to favor the decision to migrate northward. Furthermore, the now long-established tradition of communication and travel to the north helped make migration less threatening.

Transportation up and down the Gulf of California, especially in the southern region, had been greatly improved in the years after the turn of the century. The development of Mexicali's cotton industry simultaneously brought development in adjacent port towns, such as

San Felipe, where steamers from the south would unload passengers and carry freight to the cape district. Many second-stream families boarded the ships that steamed their way north loaded with contracted labor for the Mexicali region. Scores of individuals from the mainland interior also boarded steamships on the west coast at Guaymas and Mazatlán. On the Pacific coast steamers brought peninsular families into San Diego from Cabo San Lucas and San José del Cabo.

The great flow of Mexicanos into the U.S. began in the late 1920s, and although the second-stream peninsular migration can be included in it, the Baja Californios are easily distinguished. Mexicali was the major crossing point for the thousands of mainland Mexicanos who labored in the Imperial Valley and were to become the principal base of the future Mexican-American population in California. This great mass of people continued north, following the farm labor routes that scattered these people throughout the United States. In California Mexicanos first went into the Imperial Valley and then moved north to the Central Valley. But peninsular families entered the border area and remained there. Mainland Mexicanos had made long journeys from distant states of the interior and the return was equally long. But many peninsular families could return to homes and family in Mexico by merely changing residence from Calexico to Mexicali. Mexicali families kept close, often daily, ties with the "settlers" in the U.S. The network of familial relations thus became a social force that helped tie all members to the frontera region.

Beyond simply providing numbers for the growth of the greater network, the second stream regenerated hometown sentiment and communication with regions and kin in the south. As kin, the new immigrants were readily accepted into households and offered the mutual support that had become common among the earlier settlers. For many families this was a time of reunion. Separated brothers and sisters met for the first time, and *parientes* of all degrees sought refuge with experienced kin. News of loved ones and change in the south rekindled the regional bonds felt by the earlier migrants. Not only were kin seeking relatives in the north; those in the border region began sending for other kin as well. Soon aunts, uncles, and parents of immigrants were coming to the border to join their kin.

Growth of the network during this phase was also fostered by marriages between peninsulars in the southern region of the peninsula. Marriages between families in geographically adjacent towns was common and promoted a pattern of family intermarriage which continued to occur during the phases of development of the border network. While families from different towns migrated north during the mining period, became acquainted and settled along the border, southern members of the same families were united through marriage in the south. In a sense, the network had a developing counterpart in the southern peninsula. As these couples came north they often found kin in the network affiliated with both the husband's and wife's lines of descent.

Mobility at the End
of the Twenties

Mobility for network members was at its peak in the middle and late twenties as families and individuals arrived on steamers from the south via the gulf. Peninsulars went to and from San Diego on the old wooden slat road that passed from Calexico through the sand dunes of the "American Sahara," and they continued to arrive directly from the northern peninsula. The development of Mexicali and Tijuana created new employment, and families began to return to live on the peninsula again. Siblings and other close *parientes* now lived on both sides of the border, and families spread throughout the region. The daily crossing of the border for both economic and social reasons was common. People crossed freely without legal formalities. Immigration was similarly a simple transaction. Individuals merely recorded their crossing at U.S. immigration (after 1917 they paid a small legal fee of entrance; see chapter 5). The presence of family on the U.S. side made such crossings easier.[2]

The generational composition of the network began to change in this period as the passing of the first of the pioneers marked the end of a generation. Their offspring, members of the pioneer immigrant families, continued the momentum. Offspring became heads of households and made decisions based on their experience in the mines and along the border where many had lived the majority of their lives. Numerous original pioneers were still alive, but they were in the care of their offspring who had become the breadwinners. This generational change marked the movement of families into San Diego county. This move, although not collective, saw the majority of families of this study in the region before the 1930s.

SAN DIEGO–LEMON GROVE:
FLORESCENCE, 1930–1950

During the last phase of network development Baja Californios inten-sified and strengthened their community as in no other period of border settlement. This strength of community stemmed from a number of factors. When families began arriving from Calexico they received support from a group of long-settled families that had come to San Diego earlier. Furthermore, early settlement occurred primarily in Lemon Grove, a small community that served as an epicenter for local jobs as well as for continual social and family gatherings. New members from the community were incorporated into the network, and a high incidence of kin extensions through marriage and *compadrazgo* took place at this time. These kin ties formalized relationships between families for successive generations.

When peninsular migrants moved from Calexico into San Diego county, they were received by a group of families that had not lived in Calexico. In the decades between 1910 and 1930 (the Calexico-frontera phase) families from both the mining circuit and the cape region had settled in San Diego and adjacent municipalities. Among these were brothers, sisters, and family acquaintances of the Calexico settlers. These individuals first provided a base for communication about pros-pects in San Diego and later facilitated settlement. When the Calexico families packed their belongings and made their way west, they often traveled in family groups. Model T's laden with children, adults, medic-inal herbs, and immediate belongings headed toward the West Coast where siblings and other close *parientes* received them. A few families went north first, others directly into San Diego, and some went back to peninsular hometowns only to return north again. But they were all to have varying roles in forming and establishing a community of Baja California kinsmen in San Diego county.

Baja migrants and other Mexicanos were attracted to Lemon Grove, a small agricultural area about ten miles east of San Diego, because of the social environment and economic opportunities. Lemon or-chards and other agricultural fields provided the background for the growing community. There were several areas for employment, espe-cially in the lemon fields and the neighboring citrus packing house. And in nearby Spring Valley there was a rock quarry that employed miners. Many original mining circuit migrants had been employed there. In the 1930s Lemon Grove developed rapidly as an enclave of

Mexicanos. The rural environment allowed both work and social relations that were similar to those in the towns in the south. San Diego and other immediately adjacent towns provided jobs as well but did not threaten the social relations of the Californio community. Furthermore, the border, about twenty miles to the south, allowed easy return to Mexico and the home region, which, after a period of time, became the natural choice of resettlement for many Baja Californios.

The late twenties and thirties saw the solidification of the Lemon Grove community as familial relations between Baja Californios and other incorporated families prospered. The close-knit community reinforced previous familial ties, and various intermarriages between community members extended the growing network. Mainland Mexican families were also incorporated into the network along with new peninsular families. Southern peninsular migrants continued arriving, bringing news of hometowns, reinforcement of peninsular ties, and sheer strength in numbers to the border network. Visitors from hometowns were common and some people returned for visits to the peninsula during these years.

During the 1930s and 1940s multiple marriages in the county of San Diego between peninsular families and incorporated network families provided the basis of a true social-familial florescence. *Compadrazgo* relations, marriages, and the mutual raising of offspring became the principal mechanisms of network regeneration. Offspring of migrant children came of marrying age and many of these second- and third-generation settlers were tied into the network of formal and social relations. Their intermarriages created a larger base of familial relations in which individuals from families once identified solely as peninsulars and friends were now all *parientes.*

Early peninsular family members formed the core of the collective social gatherings that marked these and following decades. Marriages, birthdays, baptisms, funerals, and holidays involved huge social gatherings of kindred in which children and adults came together, reinforcing family ties and the sense of cultural community. By the 1950s and 1960s few original pioneers were still living. The community and network continued as a strong social force, but the ties to the south were dwindling. Marriages between peninsular families still occurred, but spouses often were ignorant of their common regional origins. Some individuals, however, especially those of the second stream, attempted to rekindle ties and promote visits to peninsular hometowns.

–4–

CALMALLÍ:
THE MINING CIRCUIT
AND EARLY NETWORK
DEVELOPMENT,
1880–1910

The social relations that developed on the trek north and along the border have their roots in the early history of the families that migrated north. These histories include the migration experience and the geographic locales that came to be the social settings for the first meetings and friendships of the families of the network. Most of the early mining families traveled to the placer mines of Calmallí, the town that became particularly important as the key site of interconnection for the families of this study. Family experiences in Calmallí illustrate both the primary sociocultural characteristics that formed the basis of network development and the nature of family life in the mines.

The actual migration experience of Baja Californios can be reconstructed by detailing the mining circuit experiences of three important families: los Marquez, los Mesa–Smith, and los Castellanos. Such historical reconstructions become more than migration histories. They are the histories of pioneer families that experienced foreign involvement in the peninsula, successive moves, and the hardships associated with migration in Baja California. I trace each of these families from its place of origin in order to point out their reasons for migration and the nature of life in the hometown region. The interrelations of these families in Calmallí as well as during the migration north to the border are especially pertinent. Moreover, these histories illustrate the variety of individual circumstances and responses along with the principal socioeconomic conditions of the time which led these early immigrants to the border and into the United States. The interpersonal relationships of individuals in their daily lives, in their neighborhoods, and in their work of the mines reveal the close friendships and sentiment that led to kin relations in the north.

CALMALLÍ: THE GEOGRAPHIC NEXUS

Migrant families traveled through a variety of small towns along the Baja mining circuit, but Calmallí represents the geographic and social nexus of the relationships that led to a formal kin network on the border. Some families had met in Las Flores (the Castellanos and the Sotelos) or Santa Rosalía before arriving in Calmallí; others became friends later in El Alamo, Punta Prieta, or other sites. But Calmallí was the geographic point at which migrant families began to establish social relations. Compared to other desert mines on the peninsula, the placers of Calmallí had a long production period requiring a stable working population. Here the families of this study had their longest continual contact, a major factor in establishing social relations. Social relations in Calmallí were based primarily on the mutual experience of family migration and the sharing of community life-styles. Friendships, supported by job experiences, regional backgrounds, migration, and the birth of offspring and their socialization, created the social bonds that led to close ties and relationships.

Calmallí is a desert mining town. It lies deep in the central desert almost midway between gulf and Pacific and between the cape and the U.S. border (some 450 miles north). There is no lush tropical growth here and no abundant source of water, but it is a region of rich cactus flora. Framed by the Sierra de San Borja on the east, it is within geologically new and rugged terrain. Today only ruins and bits of fragmented mining machinery remain scattered around the empty mining shafts that were opened and worked throughout the various boom days. In 1905 E. W. Nelson passed through Calmallí and described the rugged surrounding area and the southerly approach to the town.[1]

> On September 29, we made an early start and a mile beyond camp (Cerro Perdido) came to another abrupt escarpment about 50 feet high, capped by a plateau extending away eastward into the interior. Before us to our left a range of hills approached ... from the northwest, while far away to the east low mountains, some rising to an altitude of from 3,000 to

4,000 ft., stood out boldly. About 10 miles east of this last escarpment, the road led us through a range of low detached mountains of hills about a mile wide and 5 miles long. The hills rise abruptly and island-like from the level plain ... About 4 miles beyond the road led through another group of hills, turned to the south, and at an altitude of 1,200 ft. came to the mining town of Calmallí. This is located on the foot of a group of low bare hills and contained 25 to 30 small houses, two to three stores, and the reduction works for the mines. (Nelson 1922:31)

Calmallí was discovered by Don Emiliano Ibarra, who arrived in Baja California from the Alta California gold fields around 1870 (Goldbaum 1971:29). During the late 1880s an American firm bought Ibarra out and transformed the crude diggings into a company operation that produced over $3 million in gold during the most productive periods of the eighties (*ibid.*).

The stories of Loreto Marquez, a principal figure in this study, illustrate how Ibarra's role in Calmallí was kept alive by Baja mining migrants. "When we first arrived to Calmallí there was an old man Ibarra there, Don Emilio Ibarra. He worked some small ore mines, but since he had no money he didn't have the power to do anything. Then Ibarra received twenty-five thousand gold dollars for those prospects. It was a few Americans from that company in San Francisco [who gave him the money]. He had a few small holes in the ground there, and he sold" (Marquez 2/18/76:5). By the turn of the century Ibarra had sold out. The new owners, a group of Americans, were based in San Francisco, but they kept the Ibarra name for the company. The Ibarra Gold Mining Company operated into the first quarter of the twentieth century (Goldbaum 1971:29). Shipments from San Diego and San Francisco to Calmallí provided the latest in mining technology and kept the town alive.

The company saw that the mine was very rich and spent thousands and thousands of dollars to send the ships from San Francisco to the port of Santo Domingo. There in Santo Domingo [the Mexican government] sent guards and everything needed to take care of the port and the arrival of ships ... ships that arrived to unload cargo were taken care of there.

From here [in San Diego] they carried a great deal of

machinery. They put a twenty-stamp mill in Calmallí. Oh, it was grand activity! But what nonsense! It was very costly. From Santo Domingo, where the ships unloaded, everything including market goods, food, and hay for the mules was transported in; because in Calmallí there wasn't a thing.

It's about fifty miles from the port to the location of the mill. I don't know how in the world they did it. I worked in the stamp mill, but everything had already been moved there [laughing]. I don't know how they took the materials up there. Lumber, food, horseshoes, so many animals. There were about four or five wagons with six, eight mules on each wagon. Just imagine. It's the truth. Well, the mine was surely very rich; the company took out a lot of gold.

One road entered Calmallí from the Pacific landing of Santo Domingo; a rougher trail led to the gulf landing of El Barril where some materials, foodstuffs, and individuals arrived from Santa Rosalía (especially before Ibarra sold out). A series of other smaller foot trails led to Calmallí from other small mining camps, and the original El Camino Real to the north went through the town, providing a main artery into the northern terrain (Nelson 1922).

Calmallí was a company town. The population consisted primarily of company laborers and gold seekers and fluctuated with the production boom cycles of the mines. When there was no production, the town was abandoned. But during the booms the town was a center of activity. In the 1880s, during Calmallí's heyday, Goldbaum states that "there were hundreds or possibly thousands of miners living in the vicinity" (Goldbaum 1971:29). The families of this study began arriving in Calmallí in the late 1880s and 1890s and left during the down cycle after the turn of the century. During their stay there, Calmallí experienced the largest population booms and busts. By the turn of the century there were only two to three hundred miners (*ibid.*), and in 1905 Nelson reported that the area was deserted. A report of 1912 indicates that the mines were not being worked, the only population being that of cattle raisers in the surrounding area. The Mexican census of 1921 reported 44 inhabitants for Calmallí.

When in production Calmallí was a self-contained community. It was surrounded by a natural boundary of open desert and was distant from other towns and population centers. Hand-dug wells provided the only source of water and the surrounding country was no less arid. All

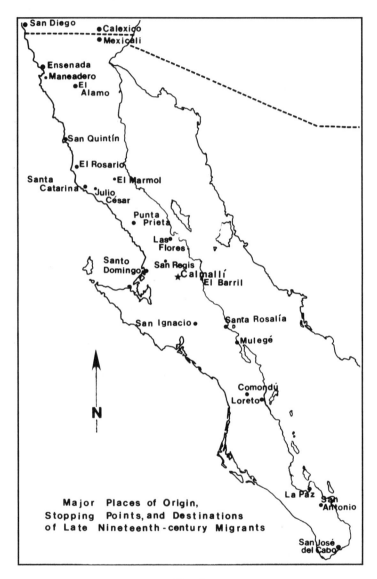

San Diego
Calexico
Mexicali

Ensenada
Maneadero
El Alamo

San Quintín

El Rosario

Santa Catarina
El Marmol
Julio César

Punta Prieta

Las Flores

Santo Domingo
San Regis
Calmallí
El Barril

San Ignacio
Santa Rosalía
Mulegé

N

Comondú
Loreto

La Paz
San Antonio

San José del Cabo

Major Places of Origin, Stopping Points, and Destinations of Late Nineteenth-century Migrants

Map 4.

social relations took place within the immediate community, for the town's isolation limited other possibilities for social interaction. As a result, individuals and families saw each other daily, worked together, and socialized after working hours. Families arriving from other mining towns and those coming from cape pueblos joined this geographically confined neighborhood. Calmallí was typical of most desert mining towns.

THE CHARACTERISTICS
OF THE BAJA NETWORK

The case studies of the Castellanos, Smith, and Marquez families, along with geographic descriptions of particular peninsular settings, are central to understanding the development of a network of social relations between the individuals as well as between the other families that participated and came to share in their mutual experiences. The importance of the towns in which these families lived seems obvious, but specific geographic influences in both migration and network development have received little attention from social scientists. The towns of Las Flores, Calmallí, Mulegé, Comondú, and other primary points where migrants lived are crucial to understanding migrant movement in the peninsula. These locales were paramount in the establishment of interfamily relations that survived any single individual. This phenomenon of long-lasting social interrelations is the basis of this study.

J. Clyde Mitchell compares the broad metaphorical interpretation sometimes given networks of social relations with more specific understandings.

> The image of "network of social relations" to represent a complex set of inter-relations in a social system has had a long history. This use of "network," however, is purely metaphorical and is very different from the notion of a social network as a specific set of linkages among a defined set of persons, with the additional property that the characteristics of these linkages as a whole may be used to interpret the social behavior of the persons involved. (Mitchell 1969:1)

I am describing a social network in a specific context. The network of Baja California consists of individuals, families, and groups of individuals. More than simple acquaintances developed over their years of migration. Strong friendships based on reciprocity, child rearing, and regional ties led to the extension of godparenthood, then marriage alliances and the birth of offspring, all of which are prime examples of the strength of these ties.

Not all the cape families that participated in this labor migration became part of the specific network I am describing. Many of these labor circuit families and individuals never continued their migration north but returned to the towns of the cape region. How long these and other families remained in specific towns is not known, and their final destinations have likewise been unidentifiable. It is probable that most turned to larger gulf towns that offered some economic opportunities, but it is also likely that some individuals returned to their hometowns.[2]

Core Individuals and Families

As in all social networks some participants are more active than others and therefore more central to the creation and maintenance of a particular social field. Such core individuals in specific social networks have not been given much attention in social science research, and the role of historical, genealogical, and qualitative social characteristics of these individuals in early development phases of social fields is usually neglected in network studies. In Calmallí such a central group of individuals became the core not only for the immediate tenure in Calmallí but also for the evolution of a larger, more complex social field many generations later. This core generated intrafamily marriages, the incorporation of other families into the social field, and *compadrazgos,* all of which became the basis of a geographically defined social community in the United States.

In this case core families and individuals are those who had similar experiences in the mines and small towns of the southern cape. The families shared close ties based on a particular regional history that placed specific towns and families in close sociocultural association. Core families kept alive the memories of those living and of migration experiences on the peninsula. The core was in this way a foundation for intrafamily cohesiveness and for the initial cross-ties of kinship that formed the basis for further family extensions of Baja Californios in the border region of the United States.

The Calmallí phase represents the initial coalescing of the core, which became the binding force of social relations despite the dispersal of families when Calmallí could no longer support a labor population. The core in this study includes eight principal families. This is a conservative number, for surviving migrants and early migrant offspring have identified over eighteen families associated with the main social field at this time. I have, however, positively identified the presence and social interaction of the eight families in Calmallí.[3] Relations of the social field, however, extended to other families and individuals in the mining community. I cannot enumerate the actual number of families and individuals participating in this specific field, but there must have been a great deal of social interaction extending beyond the core.

Along with los Castellanos, los Marquez, and los Smith, the identifiable social core also includes los Becerra, originally from El Triunfo, an early mining town south of La Paz, los Gonzales from the southern cape, los Alvarez from San José del Cabo, los Villavicencio from the Loreto area who settled and remained in Pozo Alemán just outside of Calmallí, los Bolume from the cape, los Simpson from San Antonio, and los Vasquez. Two families, los Blackwell and los Moore, from Alta California, were also part of the social field. These "families" are represented in Calmallí by groups of relatives (e.g., two parallel cousins of the same generation), extended families, nuclear families, and lone individuals.

The social interaction of these individuals derived from labor in the mines and from the interaction of households. This activity was not isolated or segmented; rather, it involved significant life-cycle experiences, including births, child rearing, adolescent development, friendship, extension of kin, and death. The sharing of these important life experiences along with participation in purely social, informal gatherings provided the basis of interaction and trust (*confianza*) (Lomnitz 1977) fundamental to network maintenance.

Confianza: The Basis of Relationships

Confianza means the general trust that develops between individuals. It is often characterized and identified by dyadic interrelations but includes a myriad of relationships. Dyadic relations are encompassed within a greater base of interrelations that stem from multiple relations between groups of individuals. *Confianza* as fundamental trust forms the basis of multiple relations among individuals within specific socio-historic settings. It is the underlying base of reciprocity of all types in both dyadic and multiple social relationships of specific social networks. This perspective differs from recent definitions that view *confianza* solely as an extension (or variable) of reciprocal exchange, in which the exchange of favors, goods and services, and information between two individuals is the prime factor (Lomnitz 1977:193). From a maximizing/optimizing (both social and economic) point of view, this is generally true. But when viewed from the historical development of particular social relations, *confianza* goes beyond any two individuals and is characterized by the interaction of individuals in a myriad of interrelations. Any single dyad or reciprocal relationship of trust can be understood better when viewed in relation to the larger complex of relationships of which it is a part. The separation of individuals into dyads permits a focus on the types of reciprocity involved, but it also leads to the exclusion of the natural relations between the dyad and others and it ignores the influence of multiple relations/myriads on any single dyadic relationship. In this study reciprocal exchange is vastly important because it is one of the identifying factors of the Baja California family network. But for this network of relations it is inaccurate to label reciprocal relations *confianza,* for the converse is the case. *Confianza* is the trust that forms the basis for the types of interrelations of which reciprocity between dyads is but one example. *Confianza* is the underlying factor in specific social contexts which produces a density of relations and aids in the stabilization, further development, and expansion of immediate social fields. In Calmallí (and the mining circuit) *confianza* was a major factor in the continuing development of social relations in the specific group of individuals that became the core to this network.

I base interactions in the core on the reconstructed histories of particular families taken from interviews with original Calmallí migrant offspring. Only one individual interviewed was an adult when in Calmallí, and he possessed specific knowledge of interaction and mutual trust among the families that made up the social core at this time. This was Don Loreto Marquez. But a number of pioneer offspring born during the mining circuit migration recalled specifics about other families and their social interactions during this phase. This direct participant knowledge, along with archival records, placed individuals and families in specific geographic locales and helped lead to the identification of family interaction. Another important source indicating family interaction was the relationships of marriage and *compadrazgo* between families and the interpretation of these formal patterns by migrant families themselves. Marriages between pioneer migrant families in San Diego after the turn of the century resulted directly from families' knowing one another in the mining circuit. *Compadrazgos* between family friends from the mining regions became common, and *compadres* often reminisced about the Calmallí days. Family ties are among the significant recollections of Calmallí. These relations stand out because they were prominent in the lives of these individuals. The experience in Calmallí was defined by these early pioneers and explained to their offspring in terms of social relations with specific families. To illustrate these relations let me return to the southern peninsula and recount the migration of Don Loreto Marquez and the familias Castellanos and Smith north toward Calmallí.

NORTH TO CALMALLÍ

The migrant experience was paramount in the lives of these individuals. Each family history traced from the hometown area presents a full representation of the regional, economic, and kin factors that influenced migration. This social history helps to illustrate how these and other families provided support to one another and created the culturally relevant relations that produced social equilibrium rather than social breakdown throughout the process.

The families described here have a number of common attributes (although before they arrived in Calmallí they were unknown to one another). They all had experience in the peninsula mines where they often met mutual friends. They all shared a regional culture and history and identified closely with many of the family names that made up that history. Each family had knowledge of other families, where they were from, and often knew individuals from these families. In Calmallí they shared their daily lives, worked side by side, and shared the important life events that brought them together as close friends and later as kin. Each of the following histories presents a rich, interwoven pattern of the particular sentiments and perspectives on working the mines, life in the towns, and relations with other families, all of which made up the migration experience.

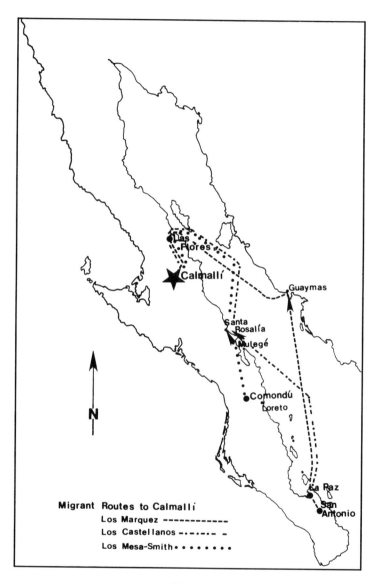

Map 5.

Los Marquez: A Mining Family

I have reconstructed the history of los Marquez from the life of Don Loreto Marquez, who followed the mining circuit and vividly recalls the days and experiences of the mines. He spent his first thirty years in the mining communities of the peninsula which form a large part of his life story.

Don Loreto Marquez was a miner by birth. He was born in 1880, the eldest of three, in the mining community of San Antonio, where his parents also had been born. San Antonio was also the birthplace of the first commercially worked mines in the peninsula[4] (Aschmann 1967:25). Don Loreto's father was a miner and the boy was initiated into mining before his tenth birthday.

We do not know when the Marquez family came to San Antonio, but it is likely that they were among the early settlers there. The Marquez line is traceable to the first successful settlers on the peninsula, and the family is said to have been one of the first Creole families. In 1679 Nicolas Marquez, a Sicilian soldier, was among the five volunteers who accompanied Father Juan Salvatierra to Loreto.

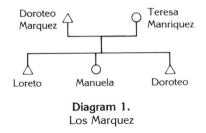

Diagram 1.
Los Marquez

In San Antonio los Marquez, like other miners, were poor, and Don Loreto worked initially to help his father support the family.

Life was very hard. Well, in those years there wasn't a thing like today. Uuuh! Today the difference is like heaven. And it was not difficult for just me but for my family and many others who lived then.

Well, we were there in El Triunfo, at that time, and to work I went. We were raised in the little town of San Antonio. The road that leads to San José del Cabo is very close to El Triunfo. The road begins at La Paz then goes to San José. Today that is a very good road. In those times there was nothing more than . . . nothing. People traveled only by foot (*a puro pie*). We walked to the top of the hills, everywhere, to work in the morning at all hours, and it rained. A person was obligated to go.

At the age of eight or nine Don Loreto was already working. He and other children were used to break up the crude ore outside the main shafts of the Triunfo mines. He vividly recalls this work and describes the technology of the period.

They kept me busy outside the mine. A young person was not allowed to enter inside. There were only grown men inside. There was plenty of machinery to carry the crude metal from the mines. Here [illustrating for me], for example, from the curb [about 25 feet] was the plain. And over there was the machinery. And here they came with a dump car. They dumped everything on the edge [making gestures to show the location and the movement of cars dumping raw ore]. With the small cart the grown men dumped the ore there. And over here they kept the younger boys like us. They had about fifteen or twenty boys there, along with an old man who watched us and told us what to do. Our job was to separate the good ore from the bad. The worthless metal we piled up [gesturing with his hands, showing how they picked up the raw metal and piled it up into two piles], you see? And the good metal we split. We always carried a hammer to break the metal into a certain size. The metal had to be small because in those times there were only a few types of machinery. The metal was taken to the smelter ready for processing because there was no rock crusher. We were the rock crusher [laughing]!

In the next twenty years Don Loreto became a permanent part of a mining labor circuit that took him to every major mine of the period. The family's migration began in the late 1890s. His father left San Antonio to work in the more northerly mines of the peninsula, then returned to get the family. They left San Antonio accompanied by another family and headed to La Paz on the Gulf Coast. The families were going to Las Flores, where Loreto's father had secured a job in the mines of San Juan. They went by steamer first to Guaymas across the gulf, then to Las Flores. Don Loreto's description of the trip tells us about company shipping, travel at the time, and the northerly San Francisco route.

> We boarded a ship in La Paz and went to Guaymas. That steamer...went along the San Francisco line and all these ports between here and there. It made a trip each month. Well, it left us in Guaymas.
>
> From Guaymas we boarded a boat from the mining company of Las Flores. The company was referred to as Las Flores, the actual mines were called San Juan. We stayed in Guaymas about four or five days...then we crossed the gulf.
>
> The Las Flores Company had a boat...they sent to all those little pueblos. It went to Mazatlán, Manzanillo, and Guaymas to pick up and send goods here to the company and material and whatever was needed in Las Flores. The owner of the boat was a Mexican...Pancho Fierro who lived in Mulegé. And he was a...he drank mezcal like water. (3/8/76:12)

Las Flores and the mines of San Juan are some five miles inland from Bahia de los Angeles on the gulf. The town is clustered in a valley forested with large cardon cacti, cholla, desert bush, and occasional ironwood trees (once abundant but now depleted because of use as fuel). Flanking both sides of the valley about ten miles apart are the steep mountains of the Sierra San Juan on the north and the Sierra San Ignacio to the south. The steep inclines of granite mountains in the distance above the flat valley floor give the valley a canyonlike appearance. Today adobe ruins, track outlines, and huge metal tumblers once used in breaking ore stand out conspicuously as one approaches the foundry site. When Don Loreto arrived, it was a bustling mine. "We got to Las Flores where the foundry was located and there was activity there. From Las Flores they sent my father to the mine at San Juan. They sent him on mules. He took us and all the baggage on the mules."

On the granite slopes of San Juan, Don Loreto, still a boy, worked outside the mine. He talks of the mines and the workings in a manner that reveals the prominent role of mining in his own experience and his knowledge of the technology of the time.

Well, we got to San Juan. My father had a job there with the company. A mine high on top of the mountain. It was very cold and, ay! it snowed a lot there. Well, he was a miner and they sent him into the mine. And us, we stayed outside to clean and break the ore.

The ore was lowered from the mountain. Well, such a mountain that I still don't understand how they finished that job. The company had put up cables with braces. [Illustrating with his hands] Here is the canyon, right? And here is mountain and over here is mountain [describing a ravine in the mountain that enters the valley floor at a right angle]. From the two sides of the mountain they placed wooden braces with a cable. It's about two or three miles long. Right in the mountain, in the actual rock! And down below . . . the ore arrived to the valley. There the ore was taken to a deposit.

The ore was lowered from the mountain in small "baskets," as they were called, small iron boxes. On the top of the mountain [still gesturing with his hands] the cable was rolled up on some huge wheels. And with only a lever here, at the base, it was controlled, so that it wouldn't go too fast, because the baskets that were loaded went very rapidly because they were very heavy. With these full baskets they pulled the empties up.

Very slowly, I'm telling you, they made the ascent, turning, turning, and turning. In that way the full ones pulled the empties. They went up and made the return.

The hacienda, as it was called, was in the valley where the foundry was located. Because this was foundry ore. Well, the work lasted. I believe we stayed . . . about three years there in the job. It ended and everything stopped. (2/18/76:3)

San Juan, like many of the peninsula mines, had a brief life. After three years, around 1895, the Marquez family packed up their belongings and headed south, beckoned by word of work in the placers of Calmallí. But their stay there was short, for, as was common in the exploitation of Baja California mines, San Juan was reopened. Don Loreto remembers the early move to Calmallí. He notes how laborers were dispersed throughout the peninsular region when company towns died: "Well, then the people began to leave to wherever they could. Some left for Mazatlán, for Guaymas, to El Palmar. At that time we headed directly through the mountains with burros . . . You should have seen those tragedies. A person walked to arrive at a water spot. We came from San Juan to Calmallí."

The Marquez entrance into Calmallí seems to have taken place before other families of this study arrived there. It is likely that some of the other families arrived while the Marquez family was there during their first stay, but the exact dates of their meetings are unknown. When los Marquez left Calmallí, they first returned to Las Flores, then went south to Santa Rosalía, only to return again to Las Flores and to Calmallí. These peregrinations occurred in a period of about six years. The round trip (Calmallí–Santa Rosalía–Calmallí), a mining labor migration, illustrates the hardships of peninsular travel. But more important, it demonstrates how families adapted to migration as part of a way of life.

> From Las Flores we went to Calmallí. And from Calmallí we returned to Las Flores because everything ended there too. But then we had already come by land, battling with the mule loads. Two or three days of travel to arrive in Las Flores, to work once again. We stayed in Las Flores on our return, living there once again. The work had stopped above in the mines [San Juan] and I don't know how much time we stayed. We worked there in Las Flores doing odd jobs.
>
> We came to Santa Rosalía and from Santa Rosalía back again. We stayed in Santa Rosalía a long time, until the work finally ended. Then we came to Las Flores. From Las Flores we went back to Calmallí again, with another company that began working for a short time until the work ended.
>
> I was twenty or twenty-one years old at that time [laughing]. I think I turned twenty in Santa Rosalía [in 1900].

Don Loreto's father left Santa Rosalía first, for work in the Las Flores mines and soon sent for Loreto and the family. Don Loreto was working at El Boleo, the French concession in Santa Rosalía when he and his family learned that their father had found work again in Calmallí. Loreto had a secure job at El Boleo, but when his father sent for them, he left. Family unification was the important factor in the move.

> At any rate, when we found out about my father, I had a very good job in Santa Rosalía. I earned two pesos a day [laughing], two silver pesos. It was a lot of money.

Yes, we had been told and we knew that my father was in Calmallí. One day as we were remembering, a man arrived with ten mules [sent by his father to pick them up]. My father had gotten a good job and was made captain of the mines, because that was his trade, the mines.

Well, I was there in Santa Rosalía, working at my job. I earned enough money to take care of the family there. My mother and my sister and "Tey" [his brother] was the whole family. Well, then, here comes this man with that army of animals. I already knew the man. His name was Antonio Espinoza.

"Well," he says, "I've come here because Doroteo sent me for all of you, to take you all to Calmallí."

Don Loreto arranged to feed the mule team that afternoon, and the following day he went to his French boss (*jefe*) to arrange for leaving and collecting his pay. "The following day we left Santa Rosalía for Calmallí. Well, that next day in the afternoon we packed everything up . . . some friends went to the house and they were really complaining about our leaving. It was a mess! 'Victor: they didn't want you to leave.' 'Yes, so many friends.'" In Calmallí the Marquez family met and became part of a social field of families that formed the basis of mutual relationships throughout the next seventy-five years of Don Loreto's life. Among these individuals and families were los Smith and los Castellanos, whose migration to Calmallí was similar to that of los Marquez. The Smiths went first to San Juan and then to Calmallí to work in the mines, but both their place of origin and their reasons for migrating were quite different.

Los Mesa–Smith: Comondú Migrants

Smith family lore is full of stories of origins that include pirates and whalers, but the Smiths of this study began with a Yankee sailor from New York City who arrived at San José del Cabo in December 1808. When Thomas Smith decided to stay on the peninsula, he became the first citizen of the United States to permanently settle in the greater Californias. Like other sailors who settled, Smith took the name of his godfather, Javier Aguílar and used it for the rest of his life. He served the presidio of Loreto as sailor and soldier and then married Maria Mesa, settling in the little town of Comondú (Crosby 1981:1–2). The family name of Smith was used again by his descendants later in the century. In addition to the Smiths, los Arce and los Mesa settled in Comondú. Descendants of the Smith-Mesas also include other families in the Comondú–Loreto kin field. These are los Green, los Collin, los Drew, and los McLish (both los Green and los Collin came to San Diego in the early 1920s). These families had arrived during the peak whaling periods in the nineteenth century.

Comondú was one of the first mission sites on the peninsula. Located in Baja California Sur, at the outskirts of the central desert, Comondú was a natural early focus of settlement because of its major source of water. The town became the major municipality encompassing the principal gulf towns of Loreto and Mulegé. The valley was known for its oasislike beauty and lush growth. "It smells of wine and olive oil. Comondú, Allah's paradise, has a stream of oil and another of wine, which metaphorically cross all the fertile land of the valley ravine where the pueblo hides. Comparing it with Eden . . . Comondú only lacks a river of milk, because here there are cascades of dates, and torrents of figs and oranges in abundance" (Jordan 1951:226).

Comondú was and continues to be primarily agricultural. The population since the turn of the century has varied only slightly. The Mexican census of 1910 gave the town a population of 1,050, and in 1920 there were 852 inhabitants. Not until 1960 does the census again give populations for localities; in that year Comondú's population was 755.[5] The hardships of the small ranchos, the lack of land for expansion in the Comondú valley, and the rapidly expanding mining boom in Baja California during the 1800s were obvious factors prompting movement out of Comondú and other small pueblos.

In 1894, the year of their marriage, Manuel Smith and his new wife, Apolonia Mesa, left the pueblo of Comondú for the mines of Las Flores. Their decision to migrate was primarily economic, but it was also sanctioned by a strong social and kin base that had been fostered by the early settlers of Comondú. This base provided the mechanisms for social stability throughout the migration process, for the Smiths as well as for other migrant families. Antonio Smith's brothers had traveled north through the peninsula and settled in San Diego county. Manuel Smith, Antonio's grandson, had been in communication with a sister, Ramona Smith de Howard, who had married an American, Charlie Howard, and was living in the mining circuit. With Ramona was her brother, Osidiano, as well. The decision to move north was thus not simply motivated by better economic opportunities. The decision was based on specific information from friends and kin as well as on the

Antonio Smith

presence of close kin who had succeeded in previous moves. There is also evidence that the Smiths had a history of migration to Alta California and back to Baja California. Family lore tells of the Smiths' coming from Alta California, from the residence of Antonio's brothers in El

Cajon. Town archives are corroborative. The following entry is from the Mulegé marriage records of 1895.

José Estrada Jr. and Ramona Smith (married) in San José de Las Flores, November 10, 1895. He is 34 years old, widower, native of El Triunfo, mason, legitimate son of José Estrada and Presentacion Garcia: both from El Triunfo; *She is twenty-three years old, native of Monterey Alta California,* legitimate daughter of José Maria Smith and Trinidad Romero, both deceased. [The latter were the parents of Manuel Smith.] (emphasis added)

These ties to the north offered security and knowledge of the area los Smith were about to enter. Further security came in the actual move out of Comondú as an extended family unit. Los Smith were not only traveling to waiting kin but were accompanied by close kin.

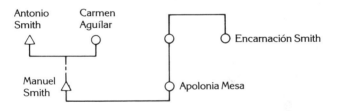

Diagram 2.
The extended kin unit of los Smith-Mesa when they left Comondú in 1894

Manuel Smith and Apolonia Mesa de Smith left Comondú accompanied by Antonio Smith, his wife and immediate family, and Apolonia's maternal aunt, Encarnación Smith. The families traveled up the Gulf Coast some three hundred miles as a kin unit, offering support and security in a manner that was to become common among families traveling between peninsular mining towns and later when they crossed into the United States. Then Antonio and Manuel took separate routes. Antonio went north to the valley of Santo Tomás. He later crossed the border into San Diego, moving to the home of his brothers, who were living in El Cajon, a farming area about twenty miles east of San Diego. Encarnación, Apolonia's aunt, remained in Ensenada.

Antonio Smith and Carmen Aguílar, who left Comondú with Manuel
and Apolonia Smith just before the turn of the century. This
photograph was taken in Ensenada in 1900.
(Courtesy of Fidel Mesa Smith)

Once in Las Flores, Manuel began working in the mines. He soon
established himself as a *leñador,* cutting, collecting, and delivering
wood for fuel used in the processing boilers of the mines.[6] Two children

were born to Apolonia and Manuel in Las Flores. Adalberto (my grand-father) was born in 1895, and a daughter, Francisca, was born shortly after. The family remained in Las Flores until about the turn of the century, then moved south to the town of Calmallí.

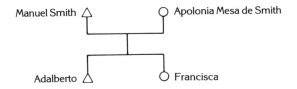

Diagram 3.
Los Smith when they left Las Flores around the
turn of the century

Los Castellanos:
Mining Circuit Friendship

The migration of los Castellanos demonstrates the usefulness of con-tinuing family ties in the northward journey of peninsular families; it also reveals the early friendships with other mining circuit families that began developing prior to Calmallí.

The Castellanos began their journey in Peru and followed the Manila galleon route north to the cape region. Slowly, over a period of fifty years, they made the trek north through the mining boomtowns of the desert. Tiburcio Castellanos landed in the cape region of Baja California in the early part of the nineteenth century and settled in the La Paz region with his wife, Juana Almenares. There they had two offspring:[7] María del Rosario and Narcisso (my paternal great-grand-father: fa mo fa). It is not certain how long the family remained in La Paz, but both Narcisso and María del Rosario entered the Mulegé district in the late nineteenth century. At the age of eighteen Narcisso married Cleofas Gaxiola, sixteen, and soon after migrated north. The Gaxiolas were a family with roots in Sinaloa and were well established in La Paz. Soon after their marriage, Cleofas and Narcisso began a northward migration. Their first child, Ramona (my paternal grand-mother), was born in Comondú in 1886. But their stay here was short, for Ramona reminisced and spoke of her early adolescence in the mining towns of the mid-peninsula rather than in Comondú itself.

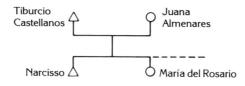

Diagram 4.
Los Castellanos when they left the cape region

Before moving into the mining circuit Narcisso and Cleofas spent some time in the Mulegé area. There María del Rosario (Narcisso's sister) had settled, having married José Estrada. This marriage linked the Castellanos not only to los Estrada but also to los Villavicencio, a large and well-rooted family in this sector of the peninsula. The Villavicencios continued close communication and ties with los Castellanos and visited San Diego some thirty years later. María del Rosario passed away in 1892 at the age of twenty-seven. By that time Narcisso, Cleofas, and Ramona had entered the mining circuit.

Like so many other families, los Castellanos went to the Minas de San Juan in the valley of Las Flores, where they met other migrant families and began establishing social relations that led to strong social and kin ties in later years. Such relations were begun with the Sotelos, a family with roots in the southern peninsula.

For los Sotelo, as for los Castellanos, their residences and prolonged stays can be determined by the birthplaces of offspring. Francisco Sotelo (Don Pancho) was born in Mulegé in the second half of the nineteenth century. He met and married Angelina Arce in San Ignacio, her hometown. Soon after their marriage (c. 1898) they entered the mining circuit and moved to Las Flores. Like the offspring of the Castellanos, Smiths, and other families, the Sotelos' eight children were born in various mining towns on the peninsula. The birth dates of the children coincide with those of children of other migrants in the same towns and indicate both the period of residence in particular places as well as the opportunities for acquaintanceships to spring up during peninsular migration. The first two Sotelo children were born in Las Flores, Teodora around 1898 and Prudencio in 1901. Guillermo was born in San Fernando, across the peninsula on the Pacific (about 150 miles northwest of Las Flores) in 1903. The family then moved south to El Marmol where Federico was born in 1905 and back to San Fernando where in 1907 Refugio was born. The family remained in the northern peninsula from this time. Francisco was born in 1912 in El Rosario and Amalia in Mexicali in 1917.

In Las Flores the two families struck up a close relationship that has continued through the 1980s. Narcisso Castellanos and Francisco Sotelo became companions and friends on the mining circuit. In San Diego Don Pancho often reminisced about their joint experiences in the mining towns: "I was the judge and my buddy Chicho (Narcisso) the sheriff." Their close ties were later formalized in San Diego, through the marriage of two of Don Pancho's daughters into the Castellanos family.

There are no clear records for the Castellanos' departure from Las Flores, but their next stop was Calmallí. The Sotelos and a host of other families also trekked south, crossed the sierra, and dropped into one of the most productive gold mines known on the peninsula.

CALMALLÍ: THE SOCIAL NEXUS

Los Marquez, los Smith, and los Castellanos arrived in Calmallí as experienced miners. They came knowing the jobs, the life-style, and many of the people supporting themselves on the mining circuit. The underlying base of all social interaction between kin and nonkin was, of course, the mining economy, which had pulled the various families together into a specific community. The permanence of these people in Calmallí led to full, meaningful social ties that later afforded a social base from which friendships and ties became paramount factors in adaptation in the U.S. These families created social environments that revolved around the work and life-style of Calmallí (and other mining sites). The long production of Calmallí provided the economic security that allowed continuous contacts between mining families who were now a permanent part of the mining economy. The mining economy was the landscape of their social environment and the basis for a life-style that became permanent in family lore. The pioneers of this study identified with the mines, with the technology of the time, and associated all of this with the social relations that evolved during this period.

Don Loreto Marquez

Don Loreto met the Smith, Castellanos, Bolume, Alvarez, and other core families in Calmallí. He remembers them as vividly as he remembers the work and its technology. The work played a great role in family relations and in the quality of life in Calmallí. Don Loreto's recollections illustrate the spirit of life in Calmallí, the miners' perspective on company labor, and the pride they took in their work.

> The first time we were there plenty of time. There were lots of people and plenty of gold there at that time. The company from San Francisco set up a very large mill in Calmallí. They spent many thousands of pesos there. Well, the mines paid out. Three or four mines that were worked silver, the crushing of the ore and throwing in quick silver. And there in the quicksilver they got the gold. (2/18/76:5)

> The mining mill was pretty far back. I believe about two or three miles. There was a wagon road, just for mule wagons. From up there, where the people were in the mines, the company carried out the ore. With machinery, I'm telling you, with "donkeys," as the machines were called. The machines pulled and there were some huge braces. The ore was taken out and dumped into some very large chutes, and from those chutes the wagons were filled. The filled wagons were then taken to the mill.

> I worked in the mill. First, I worked in the furnace where wood was used. It was a hell of a job; steam was raised to move the machinery. The work of the mill . . . nothing else. Most people have no idea . . . it's a very specific type of work, beautiful work and very costly. Because there is a lot to be done. No, not just taking the pure ore and letting water run. No!

> Here in front . . . is a type of chute where the ore falls. A piece of steel from the actual millstamp strikes and turns a small wheel as the ore is already falling inside where the stamp is striking. You see? But if too much falls—there can't be too much at the same time—the stamp doesn't rise and it doesn't work well. Because that's the way the stamp's stroke is. Each stroke is five inches, just this much, of height. It lifts only this much . . . five . . . and it drops and drops. The five stamps drop like this, almost at the same time.

Along with his pride in the mining way of life, Don Loreto demonstrated an awareness of the situation in which he and other mining families found themselves. They were company miners and had come to the mines looking for security in employment and in the social relations common to the towns of Baja California. Calmallí, like other mining towns, also attracted gold seekers and fortune hunters who flocked to the larger strikes and roamed the nearby crevices and dead streams in their attempts to strike it rich. Don Loreto talks about this contrast between company labor and independent prospecting.

> There in Calmallí ... many people worked in the mines. But for salary, understand? There were lots of people who moved over here, over there, in the small ravines searching for a little gold with small contraptions that they made themselves.
> A lot of people did that and that's how they earned a living. Many took out gold. They were lucky, they extracted little nuggets of one *adarme* [one sixteenth of an ounce]. As many as two, three *adarme*. The little gold nuggets. But not others. It was very fine gold. They had to use quicksilver.

He also remarks on the richness of the strikes: "Over where the mill was breaking the rocks, the company was extracting the gold. It was very rich, very rich. Many people succeeded [in getting some gold]. Those who were not foolish. We were very foolish because we didn't succeed. We weren't smart enough to grab even just a small amount" (2/18/75).

Don Loreto described his meeting with the Castellanos.

> R. Alvarez: It was there then, that you met Narcisso Castellanos?
> Don Loreto: Yes, in Calmallí.
> R. Alvarez: Were they already there?
> Don Loreto: I can't say for sure if they were there already. But that is where I met them. I was still very young at that time. Well, you know, when you're young you don't notice people too much. Yea ... and we worked the mines there. Castellanos, the senior, Narcisso, he was the mayordomo of the mines, of the mine laborers who worked right inside the mines. About fifteen or twenty men worked inside, you see? He was the boss and gave orders there. He was called "*capataz*" there. (3/8/76:4)

Narcisso Castellanos continually helped Don Loreto in the mines and later provided support when Loreto first arrived in San Diego. In addition, los Marquez and los Castellanos became formally tied through multiple *compadrazgo* relations in the north.

In Calmallí Don Loreto also met Ursino Alvarez (my paternal grandfather), another compadre, who worked directly under Narcisso Castellanos in the mines. Don Loreto mentions the company "neighborhoods" that brought them together.

> Ursino? I met him down there in Calmallí. In the placers of Calmallí, that's where I met him. He worked in the mine . . . the Castellanos family was there too, my father, everybody. There was plenty of work in the mines when I met him there. Well, I would see him but I was very young and I didn't know much, like when one is older. But there he was. He always came to the house, to talk, like all the working people. People met at night to talk there in the houses. That is when I met him. Later when all the Castellanos came here to San Diego, he came too . . . following his girlfriend. [Ursino wed Ramona Castellanos in San Diego.]

Families shared work and social experiences and developed the trust that became a basis for reciprocity along the mining circuit to the north as well as later in the frontera. Don Loreto met los Bolume in Calmallí. A Bolume daughter, Guadalupe, married Jesus Castellanos, and they became compadres in San Diego. The Simpsons were also in Calmallí in the late 1880s, and Don Loreto's sister (while on the mining circuit) married into another Calmallí family, los Lopez, who had also arrived from the southern cape. Los Smith and los Marquez also became close acquaintances in Calmallí. Don Loreto clearly expresses the friendship between the families.

> We met Apolonia there. That's where we came together. When I went to work I passed about twenty feet from the door of her house, to the job I was working in those times. Manuel was there. Adalberto. Adalberto was about ten or twelve years old, less, I believe. He went around with Manuel, because Manuel had burros to haul firewood to the work there. He went to the mountains, he cut firewood and . . . he took it to the company and they paid him . . . by the cord. They made their living from it.

Los Smith

The history of the Smiths on the mining circuit illustrates the formation of friendships and close ties with nonkin as well as the maintenance of home kin ties. Although other families also maintained such ties, evidence of this communication is not seen until they are in the northern section (e.g., the Castellanos received Gaxiolas and Villavicencios in San Diego during the 1920s). Los Smith, however, left Comondú with immediate kin, were received in Calmallí by kin, and aided and received kin throughout their residence there.

In Calmallí[8] the Smiths were no longer the inexperienced pueblo dwellers that had come to seek work in the mines. Manuel came as a *leñador,* a job specific to the mines which he had practiced in Las Flores. The necessity of fuel for the boilers in the mines as well as for home cooking created the small economy by which Manuel and a host of other independents became tied to the mines. Where there were mines, there was work for Manuel. Los Smith arrived in Calmallí along with their two children, Adalberto and Francisca (who had been born in Las Flores). In Calmallí a third child, María, was born.

Along with immediate family and friends like Loreto Marquez, los Smith had close kin in Calmallí. Manuel's sister Ramona was in Calmallí with her husband, Charlie Howard, an American who was working the placers of Calmallí. María, although quite young at this time, recalls visiting her Tía Ramona with whom, she says, her parents spent much time. When Ramona died in Calmallí, of complications at the birth of twins, both Manuel and Apolonia were with her. Charlie Howard left Calmallí with the twins and was never heard from by the family again.

In Calmallí the Smiths kept close ties with kin in Comondú. Letters to Apolonia's parents and sisters kept home kin in continual communication with los Smith. During Apolonia's pregnancy with María, her mother became ill and died (c. 1901). Martina and Antonia, Apolonia's sisters, knew she was in the last months of her pregnancy and wrote Manuel of the seriousness of Apolonia's mother's condition. They informed Manuel but asked that the news be kept from Apolonia, fearing for her health and the child's. This constant communication kept all kin informed about their relatives. It also facilitated the reception of kin who were on their way north as well as kin who would come north later in the century. The Mesas, for example, were received by Apolonia and Manuel Smith in Calmallí.

Ramona Smith de Howard (c. 1890), sister of Manuel Smith,
married Charlie Howard, an American working on the mining circuit.
She died in Calmallí, from complications at the birth of twins,
who were taken to the United States and never heard from
again. (Courtesy of Ernestina Ignacia Mendoza Allen)

The Mesa family migration north illustrates not only the Smiths'
hometown kin ties but also the nature and the significance of kin ties
in family migrations from hometowns into the central and northern
peninsula. Salvador and Juana (Apolonia's paternal aunt) Mesa left
Comondú, according to (their daughter) Paula, because their eldest

son had left for the north and their mother wanted to be close to him. In Comondú Salvador had packed grapes and figs destined for Santa Rosalía. From Comondú Salvador and Juana traveled to San Ignacio with six children and stayed in that mission town, where Salvador managed fruit fields (*administraba las huertas*). Although successful there, the family left San Ignacio to follow kin who had gone further north. They left in October and traveled through the central desert to the northern boundary town of El Rosario, arriving on December 3, *el Día de San Francisco*. On their way they passed through the mining towns of Calmallí and Julio César. In Calmallí Apolonia and Manuel Smith received Salvador, Juana, and the children. They stayed several days, resting, visiting, and exchanging news with Apolonia. Juana and Apolonia had been close friends and Juana was continually thinking and asking about Apolonia (so reports Hirginia, Juana's daughter). Los Mesa moved on to the north, arriving in San Quintín, where they later received los Smith when Calmallí ended production.

Among the important network relations of los Smith in Calmallí were friendships formed with nonkin. Friendships established at this time with los Bolume, los Marquez, los Simpson, and others were to have significant meaning in later years. An informal network of social relations between los Smith and los Castellanos later developed into kin ties through marriage and *compadrazgo*. A good example of one such link is Guadalupe Bolume, a close friend of Apolonia's during the years on the mining circuit. Guadalupe was born in Calmallí and later became *comadre* to the Mesa–Smiths as well as to los Marquez, and she married into the Castellanos family. This cluster of families—los Smith, los Castellanos, los Marquez, los Simpson, and los Bolume—was identified by a close friend of them all, Señor Villavicencio, who now lives in Pozo Alemán. He recalls their long stay in Calmallí and their relations as a group.[9]

Los Castellanos

Narcisso and Cleofas Castellanos were among the earliest of arrivals to Calmallí, and they spent a great deal of time in that town. When Narcisso entered the mining circuit, Ramona was an only child. By the time the family left Calmallí, six more children had been born and three others would be born in more northerly mining towns. For the Castellanos Calmallí was truly a nexus, the landscape in which specific social ties formed a basis for future marriages, *compadrazgos,* offspring, and future generations.

La familia Castellanos consisted of Narcisso, Cleofas, Ramona, Jesus, Juana, Espiridiona, Francisca, and Abel. Like other core families

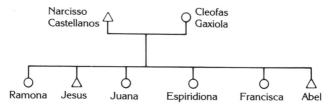

Diagram 5.
Los Castellanos when they left Calmallí

in Calmallí, los Castellanos did not actually marry during this period, but the bases for later marriages and *compadrazgo* relations were laid in Calmallí. Of the Castellanos children who grew up and were socialized in Calmallí, all of these married into Baja California families. But three married into core families. Courtships for some of these marriages began in Calmallí, as is illustrated by Don Loreto Marquez: "It was in Calmallí where I met him [Ursino Alvarez]. Later when all the Castellanos came here, he came too ... following his girlfriend. My *comadre* Ramona worked [in San Diego], I'm not sure for whom. But she wasn't married yet. She was being courted by Ursino."

Other similar courting relations developed in Calmallí and in other mining circuit towns. Guadalupe Bolume recalled dancing with Vicente Becerra, who played guitar at social affairs in the mining towns and who played for her wedding decades later in San Diego. Vicente himself was married in San Diego to Guadalupe Gonzales, who had also been on the mining trail with her parents.

Numerous marriages and *compadrazgo* relationships based on mining friendships occurred later in San Diego. Offspring of these marriages then intermarried and further reinforced the solidarity of these families in the frontera region. Overlapping formal *compadrazgos* also united families. Don Loreto, recalling Jesus Castellanos, stated, "Jesus married my *comadre* Lupe [Bolume]. Jesus, the brother of my *comadre* Ramona."

The Calmallí period, for Narcisso and Cleofas Castellanos, was not a brief interlude or simply part of a migration north. They, like the

Ramona Castellanos and Ursino Alvarez, San Diego, c. 1915

majority of others, saw themselves as permanent settlers in Calmallí. But when the mines fluctuated, they were forced to seek jobs and homes elsewhere. In many ways these individuals were locked into the mines. Narcisso, as *capataz* of *barreteros* had developed a skill specific to the mining economy, and he built his life and his family's life around that security. His children were born and raised in this environment, as were the children of the Sotelos, the Bolumes, the Smiths, the Simpsons. When the Calmallí mine could no longer support the families of workers, people moved on. Many were encouraged to head north because El Marmol, Julio César, and other small mines were producing and employing mine laborers.

NORTH TO THE FRONTERA: A PERIOD OF TRANSITION

Los Smith, Marquez, Castellanos, and other families left Calmallí when production in the mines declined. Although many migrants eventually arrived at towns on the U.S. side of the border, the march from Calmallí was a long one. Some families went to the border following El Camino Real, hitting the various mining spots along the way. Others, like the Castellanos and Marquez, went first by land, then boarded company steamers that took them directly into the United States. But even these journeys were long episodes interwoven with specific landscapes, mining towns, and social interrelations.

This period was not simply a continuation of the mining circuit; rather, it was a period of transition. The towns of the mining circuit were slowly fading from importance as fewer and fewer booms followed busts. Migrants now turned to the frontera region, whose economic sustenance derived from the development of the border towns of Calexico and San Diego. As migrants crossed the border they left not only the Mexican peninsula but also the life-style of the desert. This transition is clearly visible in the last trek of the Smith, Marquez, and Castellanos families. Los Marquez and Castellanos returned more than once to the Baja mines after crossing the border, but ultimately the mines failed and the border economy accelerated, luring families across the line to settle.

Los Castellanos:
To San Diego and Back

In addition to the collapse of the mining economy, the Castellanos gave other reasons for their northward migration. Francisca states that an American foreman persuaded them to head north. Furthermore, Narcisso, who had hired a tutor for his older children, was worried about the education of his offspring. This concern too figured in the final move to San Diego.

Narcisso and Cleofas first traveled to the small town of San Regis (about forty miles north of Calmallí) where a third son, Narcisso, was born in 1904. After his birth the family crossed the desert to the Pacific landing of Santa Catarina (about fifty miles south of El Rosario), a port that fed a variety of company towns in the adjacent interior. Francisca Castellanos (my godmother) told me of the trip, which I recorded in field notes: "Nina [my godmother, Francisca Castellanos] remembers traveling by land through the desert with the family. Most of this travel was done on burro or horseback. [She remembers that] it was hot. A guide who was with them would keep his head covered with a sheet for protection against the sun. He was carrying Chicho [Narcisso], an infant at the time" (12/17/75). "Un viejito" (a little old man), Cevero, accompanied the family from Calmallí to Santa Catarina. There at the port, along with others, they boarded a steamer, the *St. Denis,* which was going to San Diego. From shore small rowboats lightered passengers and cargo to the waiting steamer. The *St. Denis* made regular trips between the northern peninsula and San Diego, stopping at San Quintín and Ensenada before going across the international border into San Diego bay. The Castellanos arrived in 1905 and "immigrated" at the Port of San Diego.

The Castellanos' initial move across the border, however, was not permanent. In the next four years they returned twice to the Baja California mines before finally settling in the border zone. In 1906 and again in 1908 Narcisso Castellanos and the family returned to the peninsula. Both of these return trips were for the birth of children. Narcisso had insisted that all the children be born in Mexico. In 1906 Cleofas was with child and the family returned to Santa Catarina, as they had left, by steamer. From the Santa Catarina landing Cleofas, the children, and Narcisso made their way to the small mine of Julio César, some ten miles inland from the coast. There in January of 1906 a son, Tiburcio, was born. When Cleofas was well enough to travel, the family embarked again for San Diego. "As soon as my mother completed her diet we returned to San Diego" (Tiburcio Castellanos, 7/21/76). Within two years the family boarded for Santa Catarina again, this time for the birth of Ricardo. Landing once more at Catarina, the family made its way to the onyx mines of El Marmol, about fifty miles inland from the coast. That same year, 1908, the family packed up and returned to San Diego. This trip was the final one and the move to San Diego became permanent. "It was the same thing, my mother completed her diet and we returned to San Diego" (Tiburcio Castellanos, 7/21/76).

The Castellanos' return visits to the district proved beneficial because they renewed contacts with many old family friends. Los Sotelos, los Simpson, and others were still in the mining circuit. And Ramona Castellanos had the opportunity to see Ursino Alvarez, who was apparently working at the inland mine. Don Loreto tells of the romance and of the mining environment of El Marmol.

> He was courting since they were down there in El Marmol. They [Los Castellanos] were also down there in El Marmol which is in a mountain area down below San Quintín.
>
> I don't know how many years the mine lasted. They stopped

mining just like that . . . and then began again. It was a company from San Diego. A very large steamer went to the port there. The port was called Santa Catarina. It was a small pueblo with a spring. The wagons passed through there. They pulled the wagons with mules, from El Marmol to the edge of the beach. Just imagine. It took them two days. That's right.

In San Diego Narcisso and Cleofas joined other families that had traveled the mining circuit, and in turn they all received incoming peninsular families. Within the next decade the Castellanos traveled to Calexico where they reestablished numerous acquaintances.

Los Smith:
The Trek To Calexico

As Calmallí production dwindled and work there diminished, families dispersed and moved to other towns. Most went to mining sites within the central desert. Los Marquez traveled northwest along El Camino Real to Punta Prieta. Guillermo Simpson and family went farther north to San Fernando, and los Castellanos to San Regis. It is probable that many families went south and home. Los Smith, however, went north to the valley of San Quintín.

During the years 1906–1908, after leaving Comondú, Manuel and Apolonia Smith traveled at least four hundred miles. They moved to Calmallí, then followed El Camino Real through Punta Prieta, Laguna Chapala, San Fernando, El Rosario, and into the then small agricultural zone of San Quintín. In San Quintín they arrived at the home of Juana and Salvador Mesa. (Los Mesa had previously stopped in Calmallí, and although they had remained only a few months, this stay reinforced the two families' ties.) Hirginia Mesa, who now resides in Maneadero (about seven miles south of Ensenada), remembers the visit of Manuel and Apolonia. They had come very far and were looking for work. Manuel worked there during the harvest in the agricultural fields. Later Hirginia and her sister Paula ventured into the north and renewed ties with Manuel, Apolonia, and their children.

From San Quintín Manuel went further north to El Alamo, where a new strike had attracted people to the mines. But like other mines, El Alamo lasted only a short time. As contemporary reports illustrate:

On the western side of the plain, some forty-five miles south of Real Del Castillo, is the Santa Clara placer district and what remains of the old mining camp of El Alamo. Here, early in 1889, several thousand gold seekers converged, and Goldbaum, representing the government, helped to collect mining fees and give possession to claimants. (Lingenfelter 45 in Goldbaum 1971:52)

The rush only lasted a few months, however, although quartz mining continued in the vicinity off and on for many years. (Southworth 74, 89 in Goldbaum 1971:52)

In 1905 Nelson described El Alamo: "... with its vacant houses and dilapidated appearance [it was] a typical broken mining camp. There were many signs of former activity here in considerable scale, but at this time only a few men were working. New supplies were being sent in and a revival of work was being announced with the usual sanguine expectations."

In El Alamo Manuel worked the mines while Adalberto, now older, took to the *campo* (countryside) as a *leñador*. Rosa Salgado,[10] a native Paipai, Indian, who was to become part of the Smith network, recalls their arrival and also reveals the close ties that developed in the mining community.

> R. Alvarez: Aunt Rosa, did you ever meet the parents of my grandfather Adalberto?
> Rosa Salgado: Yes, I met them when they had just arrived from the south. At that time I was working for a lady.
> R. Alvarez: Where, Aunt Rosa?
> Rosa Salgado: There in El Alamo. They arrived there. They had come from the south.
> R. Alvarez: Did they stay there very long?
> Rosa Salgado: Yes, they stayed there a while because their father Manuel was working there. Ooh! There was a lot of people working there in the mines. He started working there as soon as he arrived. Working there in the mines. He had Adalberto with him ... Adalberto was very young.
> I have a brother and Adalberto came to the house and would invite him way up to the hills to collect firewood. They took

burros. My brother would go with him and bring firewood. Adalberto collected [firewood] and loaded the burro, and he would leave firewood for us too. Adalberto and two sisters came with the family. One, Maria, she's the one that's still alive, right? The other sister was Panchita. The two girls looked exactly the same. Then there was another boy. I don't remember what his name was. (6/18/76)

Apolonia had her fourth child, Manuel, here but lost a child, Panchita, who had come ill from Calmallí. While Panchita was ill, Apolonia sent her to los Larrinagas in Ensenada. They were kin from Comondú and they cared for her while they sought medical help. But she came back to El Alamo, where she passed away. "The girl didn't last the year. She got sick, I believe. I went with them when they buried her there in El Alamo. Such a beautiful girl. She had long braids, all the way to her waist" (6/18/76). The loss of Francisca played a strong role in the family's next move north. María states that this was the crucial reason for the move to Calexico. Her mother was grieving and wanted to be in another location.

Around 1914 Manuel and Apolonia went north with a stream of other families to the developing region of Calexico. Following the pattern established when they first left Comondú, they left El Alamo with a group of other families from the home region. As described by Maria, the surviving daughter, "Era una carpatada de familias" (It was a carpet of families). That included los Blackwell and other friends.

When the families arrived in Mexicali, they went directly across the border to Calexico. In 1910–1915 Mexicali was only a region of ranches and farms, but Calexico, across the line, was the center of activity for the Mexicali valley. There los Smith were reunited and received families from the south. Among these families were a host of kin who sought out los Smith in Calexico and reestablished close ties in a social cluster that merged with other mining families later.

Don Loreto Marquez: El Cajon and the Mines Again

Don Loreto lived as a miner throughout his traveling through the peninsula. In the boom days of Calmallí, as in Las Flores and Santa Rosalía, he had always succeeded in working good jobs. He learned

Los Smith in Calexico, c. 1915. Left to right, Apolonia Mesa-Smith,
Jesus, Manuel, and Adalberto. (Courtesy of
Flora Fernandez de Smith)

skills that he used in mining as well as later in life. He learned black-
smithing and he worked in the foundries of various towns. Around
1905, when he left Calmallí, it was not solely a departure from a job
and friends. The move marked a transition into the north that would

take him and his family into the United States and that would present a new and different way of life.

The move north for Loreto Marquez was slow, as for many other individuals. He first stopped and worked in the Punta Prieta mine, which died a quick death. Forced to work elsewhere, he went to San Quintín around 1909. Then, like the Castellanos, he headed to San Diego. This initial move to San Diego was not permanent and the old life in the mines beckoned him. He returned to the mining circuit with an old "boss" and remained for six years before returning to his parents in San Diego county. The hardships of the mining life are clear in the Marquez case.

I came here to San Diego first in 1910. My sister . . . was already here. She had come from the mine down there in Punta Prieta. But we stayed there in Punta Prieta, me and my brother, my mother and father. But there was no work. We were there in the desert, that's it.

When the work ended we stayed in Punta Prieta. We were there, moving over here and over there looking for any little pebble to survive. The boss gave us whatever he could get. He came from Ensenada and brought whatever little thing in the boat. And he maintained us there. I don't know what they did with the mill after the company abandoned Punta Prieta.

When they put the mill up, it was an eight-stamp mill, that's all. It was very small. The company wasn't able to work any longer because they spent so much to put up the mill. It was very costly and a lot of work.

The company brought an engineer, a German, who had been the engineer in the Port of Ensenada. He got along with everyone there. My boss, Brown, took him to Punta Prieta. And that German put up the mill. Flick was his name. Flick . . . big as hell. He was a very good person, that's for sure. Remember that when the work ended they all went to the United States. The German came up here to Los Angeles; he had a job to do around there. But we stayed there in Punta Prieta without work.

When the boat from Ensenada arrived . . . they brought us a letter for my father. The German . . . got a contract in San Quintín and he wanted my father to send us there to work with him. San Quintín is located below Ensenada. (2/18/76:13–14)

The valley of San Quintín lies approximately 190 miles north of Punta Prieta on the Pacific Coast. Along with Ensenada, the town had been a major northern port of trade during the nineteenth-century otter trade; it later became a major agricultural experiment. First owned by Americans, then later by a British company, San Quintín was converted into a wheat-growing district. A large flour mill was built and dry farming of wheat was practiced for many years. Mexican, English, and American colonists began settling the region, but successive droughts brought doom to the colony. Well-conceived plans for a northern connecting railroad, for which some track had already been laid, died along with the crops.

The mill, railroad tracks, and other machinery were all that remained of the venture, and a crew was hired to dismember the mill and salvage all that was possible. Don Loreto and his brother, Doroteo, went to San Quintín as part of the salvage crew.

Well, there had been a flour mill in San Quintín, but I don't know when. A very rich company from England, owned by an Englishman, planted who knows how many sacks of wheat there. There are beautiful lands in San Quintín close to the water marsh. They built good houses and everything; they put in a train that was to go to Ensenada. They wanted to reach Ensenada with the train, to haul the flour and everything . . . Well, I'm not sure when that was because that is what people said. I don't know because I wasn't there at that time. But when we arrived, people told us that when the mill was in full swing they milled flour. We came because the German, Flick, got the contract to dismantle everything there.

Well, the German sent a letter to my father that he should take us to San Quintín to work there with him. He already knew me and my brother. Well, after we opened the letter . . . my father looked for some mules right away. He brought them and left them in San Quintín. It took us two days of traveling [about 192 miles] from Punta Prieta to San Quintín [laughing]. On mules!

When we arrived . . . he gave me and my brother a room and everything we needed to work. He had about ten or twelve men working, razing everything . . . dismantling and taking everything out.

Don Loreto stayed in San Quintín with the crew for six or seven months until the work was done. He worked as a blacksmith, making tools and various parts for disassembling machinery and for its shipping. Once the work was done, Don Loreto tells how the parts were loaded onto barges and hauled by small steamers out to a ship that would carry it all away.

> The big ship that the company sent to pick up all the machinery stayed anchored outside . . . where it was deep; a ship of immense size. It came to pick up everything . . . from the shore two small steamers pulled the cargo by barge. They made only two trips per day . . . (2/18/76)

> The ship took all the machinery that was inside the mill and the railroad track and platforms. [Laughing.] It took everything in only one trip! (2/18/76)

Once the work was finished, Don Loreto and his brother went north to San Diego, in 1910, and sent for their parents. The decision to move north was instigated by their boss, Mr. Flick, who had planned to take both Loreto and Doroteo to Los Angeles. But Don Loreto's immediate supervisor suggested that San Diego, where they had family, was a better destination. So they decided on San Diego, where they immediately sought out friends from the mining circuit.

> We came in the *Bernardo Reyes* to Ensenada. We stayed there just four or five days with some acquaintances. From Ensenada we came here to El Cajon. My sister already lived here. She was the married one. (2/18/76)

> When we arrived to San Diego we went to the home of los Castellanos. Narcisso Castellanos lived here, the father of the Castellanos who are from San Diego. He was already living in San Diego. We arrived there because he had always been very good to us and we were very close from down in Calmallí. . . . (2/18/76)

Loreto's old mining friend, Narcisso Castellanos, received them and took them out to El Cajon where Don Loreto's sister was living. Once settled the young men sent for their parents. Their mother and father also arrived on *El Bernardo Reyes,* never to return to Baja

California again. Don Loreto, however, was back in Punta Prieta before the year was out.

Life in the United States was not easy for many of the new immigrants. For Don Loreto, like others, the work was demeaning and the pay was bad, as he himself states:

And I didn't like it. The work here payed very poorly, very poorly. It was $1.25 a day. I worked with the water company of the district of La Mesa ... you heard me mention that company ... I worked making ditches with only a pick and shovel. For one dollar twenty-five [laughing]. A person threw his soul into that work. But I had very good work in Baja California with the boss, Mister Brown, who ran the business in Punta Prieta. Well, anyway I didn't like the work here, but I kept it up because my father and mother were here ... They also came after we did on the *Bernardo Reyes.* (2/18/76)

San Diego in the early decades of the century was the major business center of both Southern California and the northern frontera. The small steamers commuted regularly between the Pacific port towns and a few went as far as the cape and across to the mainland. San Diego was still a major outfitter and center of negotiations for the business and mining efforts of the northern peninsula.

On a Saturday outing in San Diego, Don Loreto ran into his old boss's son, Kenneth Brown, who advised him of a new job his father had taken in Punta Prieta. Before the day was out, Don Loreto had contracted to work for Brown again.

I went to San Diego one Saturday night. Well, who for all my great sins, while I was in the store, I ran into my boss Brown's eldest son, Kenneth [Brown had two sons and three daughters] who was walking around the stores making purchases when I was shopping for shoes or I don't know what, when I ran into him there.

"What are you doing here, Loreto?" said Brown's son, the boss's son.

"Well, nothing, I came to look around," I told him.

"Listen," he says, "do you want to go to Punta Prieta?"

"What am I going to do there?"

"My father is going again to work the mines. We're getting

ready," he said, "loading the ship and it's going to leave in three days, the ship to Punta Prieta. Do you want to go?"

"Yes," I said.

That's how I responded. That "yes." And no one here in San Diego knew anything.

Then . . . he asked me: "Don't you want an advance?"

"Yes," I said. "Why not?"

Well, there we go.

"My father has the office close to the Grand Hotel. That's where he has an office. Let's go over there."

We went there right away and I greeted the boss, Brown. And Kenneth told him, "Loreto is going with us too."

"Oh yea, that's good," he said.

Then he gave me a thirty-dollar advance. Well, I was rich. In those days everything was cheap.

That same day, in late 1910, Don Loreto purchased his gear, then went to his old friend Narcisso and advised him of his return to Punta Prieta.

"Hey, listen, Chicho."

"What are you doing here?" I told him the whole story.

"Ah, that's good," he said.

I told him, "I'm going to El Cajon. And tomorrow I'll be back and I'm going to leave this suitcase here."

"Sure," he said.

Boy, I'm telling you. I came home in the early morning so that my father could see me. And ooo! He got madder than hell . . . He got very angry. He didn't want me to go. "No, I'm going to go," I told him. "The work here isn't worth it. I'm going to work for Brown." Well, if he wanted or didn't, in the morning that next day, I left. I went to San Diego on a small train that passed by El Cajon, early in the morning. And there I went, and that's how I left. (2/18/76)

Don Loreto returned to Punta Prieta with Mr. Brown where he worked for about two years. In Punta Prieta he married Ramona Rubio and then, along with Brown, went to the island of Cedros. On Cedros Brown had been contracted as manager of a copper mine. But the

Loreto Marquez in El Cajon c. 1950. He turned twenty in 1900 while working in the El Boleo mining concession granted to the French in Santa Rosalía. (Photo courtesy of María Marquez and family)

work there lasted only a short while (two years) and Don Loreto soon returned to the border again. His wife gave birth to their first child, and for their safety Don Loreto sent them to San Diego. He later joined them in 1914. Once back in San Diego, Don Loreto never left again for the south. His mining days were over, but for the next half century his closest friends continued to be those families he had met in Calmallí and the mining circuit.

The migration of los Smith, Castellanos, and Marquez through the mining circuit, from Calmallí to the frontera region, illustrates the beginning of the social relations that formed the basis of a network that was to last through the next half century. The life-style of the mines and the geographic points within the migration north formed a social landscape that was the basis for the interrelations of families and individuals making their way north. Throughout this migration these families demonstrated an internal social order that despite constant uprooting became progressively stronger as a result of the migration experience. Close ties were formed with new friends and kin, ties that outlasted even the first generation's offspring.

Various factors, including conditions in home regions, economic opportunities created by the mining booms, and changes in mine productivity, influenced the families' decision to move north and then across the border. People did leave the southern peninsula for better economic opportunities, but such moves were sanctioned by kin and friends who traveled with or received migrants in the host communities. Furthermore, in mining towns new relations were created providing greater security and further inducement for later travel north. As people traveled north, the desert towns and the work and social communities of the mines became a way of life, important in securing and producing new relationships. Calmallí was not just another mine, it was the mine and community where families met, shared births of children, social events, and friendships.

The final move to the northern border marked the end of the mining migration. Once established along the border, these families remembered the mines of the central peninsula, like their hometowns in the cape, as places important to their families for social relationships and as a basis for a shared recognition of historic, geographic, and social ties.

– 5 –

SAN DIEGO
AND CALEXICO:
THE FRONTERA AND
EARLY NETWORK
FORMALIZATION

Once in the frontera region, many of the mining-circuit families crossed the border and settled in the United States. Settlement, like the migration north, was a long process. People moved between the towns of San Diego, Calexico, and Mexicali in their adjustment to the rapidly growing economy there. The frontera towns offered new jobs and life-styles different from the migrants' previous experiences on the peninsula. But Baja Californios not only adjusted to the towns, they created a total sociocultural world that became the basis for adaptation and settlement.

The arrival of Baja migrants in the frontera illustrates how families extended mutual help to kin ties to create a formal kin network along the border. The primary basis for this reciprocity was the institution of family sentiment, or *parentesco*, which along with *compadrazgo* (compaternity) and marriage, was used to recruit and extend ties among frontera migrants. Although *parentesco*, like *compadrazgo* and marriage, was commonly practiced in Mexico, these institutions became the basis for cultural maintenance, social adaptation, and successful settlement in the border towns of the U.S. Unlike kin extensions in Mexico, the kin ties of the border were based on a *parentesco* that included the migration experience, the regional affiliation, the mining circuit, and settlement in the frontera.

In addition to the mining circuit migrants, other peninsular migrants arriving in towns on the border contributed to the family network. These others bypassed the mines and came north primarily by sea. Small groups had begun arriving in San Diego in the early 1900s

(1905–1915) and made up a strong contingent in the Californio community in that town. They arrived from the cape region via the regular steamship lines of the San Francisco and San Diego trade. Both the early miners and these early steamer migrants provided a major base for further growth and social solidification among the Baja Californio migrant population.

Another inducement and strength came from the second stream of migrants who began arriving in the 1920s. This second stream headed north via gulf steamers to the Colorado delta during the Mexicali cotton boom. Case studies of early steamer migrants and the second-stream migrants illustrate how regional and kin ties provided a basis for settlement in the frontera.

PARENTESCO: A REGIONALLY BASED KINSHIP

Parentesco includes the recognition of kin ties between members of consanguinally extended kindreds, but the term can also be expanded to include nonkin as well. Baja Californios in particular extended the reciprocity usually reserved for recognized kin to nonkin who shared the migration experience and a historic bond associated with geographic origins. On the one hand, this sentiment was extended to migrants because of their mutual experiences and their knowledge of hometown and home region families. On the other hand, the institution of *parentesco* became a method of creating reciprocity and kinship solidarity among incoming families.

The nature of the small pueblos and close-knit populations in the south provided migrants with the social base for a potential web of interrelated kin from the southern peninsula. The small hometowns were associated with particular founders and specific families who had settled and intermarried over time. The geographic closeness of towns, as well as the isolation of the few pueblos, aided in the easy identification and association of towns and families within larger townships in the south. People in the south often traveled between their homes and the gulf, meeting other townspeople and creating friendship ties. These ties in turn often resulted in marriages that united families from different pueblos. When the individuals of this study began to move north, they recognized a wide web of southern town-family associations, which became a base for regional affiliation and the extension of familylike support on the border. In this case the close relationships of Baja

Californio families and the sturdy geographic and historical bonds between families created a base for the use of *parentesco*. But *parentesco* as used in the frontera was a broader concept than that understood in hometowns, where *parentesco* was reserved for kin; it could be expressed on the basis of regional affiliation, the migration experience, or mutual settlement in a foreign environment. Families were not just extending *parentesco* to other migrants; they were extending *parentesco* to families and individuals who shared a specific history in the southern peninsula. In this way *parentesco* acted to promote mutual aid and solidarity among Baja Californios.

The role of *parentesco* in the Baja network can be compared with the role of territorial descent groups in which membership is so defined. Goodenough's description (1970) of such descent groups in Kentucky sheds light on the use of *parentesco* among Baja California migrants. In Kentucky mountain towns, community members (as distinct from outsiders) were recognized as those individuals who had at least one parent who was a member and who also traced membership back to the original settlers from whom all members were now equally descended. In the case of Baja Californios membership in the frontera community was based on recognized descent in families from towns in a specific region of the peninsula. This recognition, along with the migration experience and the settlement in the border, provided a basis for a new expression of *parentesco*. *Parentesco*, like *compadrazgo* and marriage, became a mechanism for extending mutual help and reciprocity while solidifying the social relations for community along the border. The frontera zone with its particular cultural and social character also helped encourage the expression of regional and historic ties as well as the extension of kin institutions.

Parentesco here is not a description of the actual network links between families but rather a description of a process that brought individuals into a familial network; it is an expression of sentiment which provides support. When individuals were recognized as *parientes,* they were (and continue to be) incorporated into the social field of regional families.

My own recognition by all individuals I interviewed for this study is an example of the expression of *parentesco*. I was accepted immediately by various branches of families who were connected to the network of families in the frontera. Many of these families were actually related kin, but often they were not. On one occasion in 1975 I was talking with Chicho Hollman when he suggested we walk over to meet another Baja Californio who had arrived in San Diego in the early decades of the century. When I was introduced to Señor Ramon Martinez, he immediately greeted me as a fellow Baja Californio because of my family's background and peninsular place of origin: "You're from Baja California and we're kin. I knew Ursino Alvarez and all the Alvarezes in San José del Cabo."

In this sense *parentesco* incorporates the idea of family as expressed by Larissa Lomnitz in her study of the Gomez family of Mexico City.

> The "family" is not a kindred, though it might be defined as one segment of the kindred of an ego. It is not a lineage, though many of its members may be traced to a common ancestor. Membership in the "family" is conditioned on mutual *recognition* as such: it is expressed by a relatively high intensity of exchange of information, of goods and services, and in some cases women, i.e., endogamy (Lomnitz 1978:3; emphasis mine).

For Baja Californios in the towns of Calexico and San Diego a continuously existing network of relations was recognized. The existence of family social fields immediately provided membership in the network for any individual from included families. Knowledge of family, in-laws, godparents, and godchildren of close kin provided an open field in which family solidarity was expanded and called upon in the new environment of the frontera.

LA FRONTERA: A NEW ENVIRONMENT

Northern Baja California of 1900–1920 was a frontier territory characterized by rapid growth and an Anglo and Hispanic cultural interface. Tijuana was part of the municipality of Ensenada and, like Mexicali, was only a rural ranch area. San Diego and Calexico were bustling economic centers unlike any town on the peninsula. There was a prominent early Californio and Mexican population, and the Hispanic heritage of the Californias was evident everywhere. Yet the American ideology played a dominant role in the social environment.

San Diego was a metropolis of some 40,000 people. Activity on the port, new construction, road building, agricultural development, and the general economic support such growth dictates provided a variety of different job opportunities throughout the county and supported a booming population. Unlike the mine towns, San Diego was no single-economy town. Capitalist ventures were wide ranging. The "new town" plan of San Diego's official founder, Alonzo Horton, and the Spreckles family real-estate and railroad plans became the driving force for the "city in motion."[1]

The Mexicano migrants found themselves in an Anglo-American society. It is true that San Diego was historically tied to the peninsula, but the Spanish and Mexicano populations had always been small and centralized in "old town," which by the turn of the century was only peripheral to the new wave of construction and growth. The majority of the population was Anglo-American. San Diego was made up of new settlers attracted by the real-estate booms, eastern capitalists eager to make their own city, port developers, and a variety of native and transient individuals wishing to partake in the obvious boom of the bustling port city. San Diego was the capitalist's dream—the gateway to Mexico, the South Pacific, Panama trade—and it boasted a wealth of natural resources. Fishing along the coast had attracted a colony of Chinese fishermen whose junk fleet was stationed in San Diego. English and German steam companies made San Diego a principal port of call, and agriculture was a prosperous business for the Chinese as well. Small mining booms of semiprecious ore were common in the surrounding country. San Diego was truly a frontier city marked by a rapidly changing population and physical profile. A new port, a connecting transcontinental line to Los Angeles, and a "new town" were built while a variety of small residential areas were being opened in and around San Diego.

The frontera was a new environment for the families of this study, but it was approachable. Peninsular Mexicans were familiar with border policy through family ties and experiences in the frontera of Southern California. For some migrants the move was doubtless a totally new venture, but even those individuals knew about the north through contact with friends and kin who had been in San Diego. The steamship lines of the northern mining companies and the regular trade routes from Alta to Baja California provided continuous exposure for the small pueblo dwellers of the cape and gulf. Periodic contact with family and friends who had migrated and the historical relations of the Californias were the basis of the regional bonds felt by twentieth-century migrants to the frontera. Furthermore, hometowns were relatively close. The history of contact between the Californias and the proximity of peninsular pueblos to the border also reduced the threat of separation. Regular transportation made hometown regions accessible and migrant travel to the frontera and back to hometowns was not rare.

Although the actual crossing of the border was only a formality, settlement in San Diego and Calexico was qualitatively different from the settlements migrants made on their way through the peninsula. When the migrants left the mines and the southern peninsula, they were no longer to be thrust together in small geographically isolated communities where face-to-face meetings were daily experiences. Furthermore, the peninsulars were no longer part of the dominant population; they were a subordinate group participating in a new cultural interface. Moreover, families were often dispersed; they were not kept together by jobs in a small mining community. It was not uncommon to find migrant friends working together in the U.S., but on the whole migrants worked at various jobs and lived in various areas.

Another disparity appeared in the skills individuals brought with them and the employment they took in the U.S. Many migrants found their skills unmarketable in San Diego. Most migrants were faced with the prospect of new jobs in new fields. Skilled workers as well as ranchers and miners were no longer secure in their job experience. In the frontera many individuals were forced to undertake unskilled labor or jobs not directly related to their previous employment. All work in the small desert communities had been dependent on the mining economy, and individuals viewed their work as contributing to the success of the mines. But jobs in San Diego were often viewed as unimportant, requiring no real skill. Many of the early migrants worked in construction or picked crops, moving between jobs that often had no uniformity.

Baja mining migrants did have some preparation for the new environment. The mining experience had also presented them with a changing geographic and social environment. Individuals and their families had been conditioned by the boom-bust cycle to domestic change and adaptation to different communities. Although there had been continuity in the employment and social situations, families had participated in small, bustling economies in which Americans, English, and other non-Mexicans played a part. Many of these families, in fact, like the Smiths and Bolumes had genealogical ties to Europeans and Americans. Hence the face-to-face contact with the predominantly Anglo population in San Diego was not entirely foreign.

Individuals followed a specific pattern of entrance into the San Diego community, tracing kin and friends to their communities and then settling nearby. As in the migration to southern mining towns, miners and steamer migrants went first to the homes of their kin and compatriots, intending to settle close to these individuals. When close settlement was not possible, the assistance of the family and friends in finding jobs and support became a principal mechanism in fostering strong social relationships between peninsular migrants.

Along with the broad external forces influencing the migrants, such families in San Diego also experienced internal changes. The families themselves were in a state of transition. A new generation had been born along the mining circuit, and many had been socialized and enculturated into the life-style of the peninsula. While these individuals may have spent their formative years in the central desert, the youngest were now growing up in the frontera towns of the United States.

THE BORDER AND IMMIGRATION

Immigration laws in the first decades of the twentieth century allowed easy movement of Baja Californios into the United States. There was no border patrol, and the quotas and head taxes imposed on nonwestern immigrants did not apply to Mexican immigrants.[2] Crossing into the United States was a mere formality. Immigrants were required to register at an official port of entry. There were no other requirements. In 1917, along with registration, a head tax of $8 and photos were required of all incoming aliens. This fee was collected from heads of households, but children under sixteen were exempt when accompanied by a parent. This law, however, was interpreted loosely. The $8 fee often went uncollected, especially in the case of groups of contracted laborers headed to the northern regions of the United States.

In 1924 a number of legal changes affected the influx of Mexicans into the United States. Throughout the twenties, Congress debated the imposition of quotas and fees on immigrants entering the United States. The entrance of aliens had begun to draw attention because of the large numbers seeking employment in the developing industrial and agricultural regions north of the border during the decade after the Mexican revolution. In 1924 the border patrol was created, and in that same year immigration officials began strict interpretation of the 1917

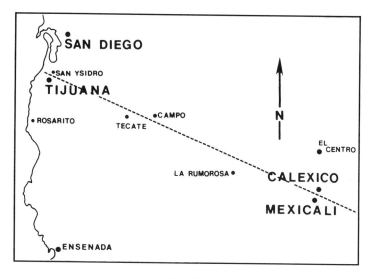

Map 6.
La Frontera

law. Mexican immigrants were refused visas in growing numbers, and the large influx of Mexicans was curtailed for a short period.[3]

The Baja Californios of this study entered the United States before this "crackdown" period. Most had arrived during the first two decades of the century when registration was the only requirement for legal entrance. There were no penalties for illegal entrance, no policing of the border, and any Mexicans apprehended for failure to register were merely told to register at official immigration stations (Hoffman 1974:11).

In the years immediately after 1924 loopholes in the law permitted entrance to some individuals. Entrance was usually allowed if immigrants had entered the U.S. previously or if they had relatives who were citizens and who could vouch for them. The interpretation of the laws was left to the discretion of immigration officers at the border. Baja Californios had a definite advantage because many had crossed earlier, most had family and friends living in the United States, and they understood the process of crossing the border.

This relatively flexible border policy reflected the regional ties between the Californias and the interrelations of the population residing on both sides of the border. The many crossings of Baja Californios from the peninsula into the United States illustrate the mobility of individuals within the frontera zone which was fostered by U.S. immigration policy at the border. The flexibility and openness of the border encouraged a constant mobility between U.S. and Mexican towns as well as the settlement of individuals from the same families on both sides of the border.

Peninsular immigrants thus easily crossed the border and entered the United States legally in San Diego, Calexico (the major border station in California), or a number of small official stations located at interior points in the United States. When the Castellanos family returned to San Diego from Mexicali in 1920, Ursino Alvarez met them in San Ysidro. The immigration offices were closed, but the family was allowed to enter the United States, where they spent the night, and return to register at the border the following day. Such actions were common during the early crossings. Los Simpson arrived around 1910 from the mining circuit at the border near Campo, a small town some forty miles inland from San Diego and about ten miles into the United States. The family went inland to Jacumba where one Mexican official took care of their papers, then they continued on to Calexico. This was the only interior immigration check station. Immigrants were expected to report to the naturalization service there to register and pay the $8 entrance fee. At that time there was no station at Tecate, the present interior crossing point.

Crossings on the gulf side of Calexico were equally easy. Martina Mesa (sister of Apolonia Mesa de Smith), who arrived with her family and her sister's family in 1920, described the Mexican and American sides as "lo mismo" (the same). The crossing procedure at that time was to go first to the border station. From there individuals were directed to the Mexican consul in Calexico, where they were asked a variety of questions and registered. Then papers were arranged. In Señora Martina's case, she and her sister along with their children were told to return that same day with the papers filled out and with photos and the registration fee. In order to pay the fee they worked that same day picking cotton, then returned and registered as legal U.S. immigrants.

The Hollmans' crossing was similarly unrestricted. In November 1910, when the "revolutionaries" came into Mexicali, Marcos Hollman took his family (at night) into Calexico, fearing for their safety. There was no immigration check, but the following day he registered the crossing with the U.S. immigration service.

Family settlement on both sides of the line also reflected early border policy. Many individuals lived in Calexico but worked in Mexicali. When the Castellanos first arrived in Calexico, Narcisso obtained a job with the Mexican government and commuted to Mexicali daily. Even Calexico advertisements for commerce and investment were directed at the growing Mexicali development.

These examples illustrate the geographic mobility of families living in the frontera zone as well as the open-border attitude expressed by the U.S. Immigration Service in the early decades of the twentieth century. Migrants approached the international line confident that they would cross the border, temporarily or permanently. Even when individuals did not have enough money to pay the fee, there was immediate work available, or family and friends residing on the U.S. side could provide assistance. I have recorded only one instance of a family's being refused entry into the United States, the cause being the severe illness of one family member. This open-border attitude greatly facilitated the continuing ties with hometowns and allowed a continuous influx of Baja families into the border zone of the United States.

The new cultural environment created an atmosphere that fostered the maintenance of kin networks and the establishment of new family interrelations. As migrants arrived in Calexico and San Diego, faced with new sociocultural conditions, they naturally sought out friends and attempted to maintain the institutions that were a part of their way of life. Stimulated by the presence and continuing arrival of other peninsulars who shared origins and migration experiences, migrants generated and extended traditional patterns of social organization. *Confianza, compadrazgo,* and marriage formed a set of kin institutions resulting in increased family interrelations. These relationships helped create an identifiable social organization of migrants in the U.S. The use of this set of kin institutions helped migrants maintain their cultural identity. The network formed a well-defined social field characterized by clear social-cultural boundaries. Family institutions became the principal mechanisms in the creation of a social kin network that provided successful cultural maintenance and adaptation in the frontera cities.

The network I am describing was not simply an extension of village networks but a more encompassing structure that was created along the border, using traditional family institutions. Village networks among migrants are characterized by interrelations between extended kin and friends who share a specific hometown (Butterworth 1970; Bruner 1973; Doughty 1970; Friedl 1959, 1964; Lewis 1952, 1973; Mangin 1973). The Baja network on the frontera included migrants from a variety of peninsular towns; it was thus a regional network that included families from a large area of Baja California. Many of the families were unknown to one another before migration, unlike the pattern with village networks, but mutual aid and reciprocity between members became common in the frontera.

When cape families arrived in San Diego, many had kin and friends who extended the support often given only by kin. These kin interactions based on particular towns were maintained when possible by these early migrants and served to bring kin in a second-stream migration during the 1920s and 1930s.

Particular hometown networks did not remain isolated kinship structures tied to home villages. The stage migration fostered expanded interrelationships between families in which home kin networks were also mechanisms for growth. When migrants reached the border and began settling, friendships, *confianza,* and early *compadrazgos* were the base for continuing relations. The frontera environment encouraged the ongoing expression of *confianza* and the extension of family institutions between families. This resulted in marriage ties and finally in a succeeding generation of offspring who traced descent to a variety of peninsular villages. In the simplest outline, mutual aid and reciprocity led first to *compadrazgo* relationships and then to marriage ties among offspring of the mining pioneers and of the (early) Pacific and gulf migrants.

The beginning of formal relations between families can be clearly seen among the early steamer immigrants. The early steamer (and mining) migrants first arrived in San Diego and formed a nucleus of Baja Californios. As Calexico grew and attracted labor, many of these San Diego entrants traveled east to Calexico, where both old as well as new ties were established. A brief synopsis of the migration of Nicolás Ceseña, los Lieras, and los Hollman families reveals the pattern of previous family migrations, the settlement in the frontera, and the early friendships and marriages that led to the beginnings of a formal border network of family interrelations among Baja Californios.

SAN DIEGO, 1900–1920:
THE EARLY STEAMSHIP MIGRANTS

Nicolás Ceseña

The experience of Señor Ceseña and his family illustrates the continuous ties maintained by families as they moved from the south to the frontera region. Sr. Ceseña's migration within the border zone and his friendship and marriage within the migrant network typifies the pattern of settlement in the early decades of the twentieth century.

The Ceseña family has a long history of mobility in the Californias. Nicolas Ceseña's parents traveled frequently to Alta California. His mother (Jesus Castro) had lived several years in San Francisco before returning to the cape where she wed Eugenio Ceseña, who traveled often to the north doing business. He shipped citrus to San Francisco and imported apples from the north. In 1898, at the age of four, Nicolás, his siblings, and his parents boarded a steamer and headed to Ensenada, where a maternal uncle and maternal grandmother had settled. His mother's brother and other relatives who had migrated earlier were living in San Diego. Los Ceseña visited San Diego often during their years in Ensenada. In 1907, when Sr. Nicolás's parents died, he was sent to live in San Diego with his uncle. He returned twice to Baja California in the next eight years, staying long enough to lose his U.S. immigrant status. But he regained it when he went to work with the San Diego and Arizona Railroad. His railroad days lasted until 1925.

During his work with the railroad Sr. Ceseña (living in Tecate) frequently visited San Diego and became close to the Baja California families. In 1919 he wed Luisa Chavez, a direct descendant of los Smith of Comondú (Luisa's mother was a Smith). Their first son, Manuel, was born in Tecate in 1920. By 1922 they had settled among a set of Baja families, residing as a community, in Lemon Grove, just ten miles outside of San Diego.

The period just before settling down was one of transition for Sr. Ceseña. His pattern of movement along the frontera fluctuated like that of los Castellanos and Loreto Marquez. But during these years families were meeting and forming a new community in San Diego. These interrelations were not based solely on new acquaintances and kin ties. Hometown ties as well as knowledge of and friendships among nonrelated families also provided a strong basis for interrelations. The lives, migration, and marriage of Antonia Nuñez de Lieras and Pepe Lieras is one such example.

Los Lieras

In 1908 Señora Lieras and her father boarded a steamer at the small port of La Palmilla[4] in San José del Cabo and went directly to San Diego. During the next nine years Antonia Nuñez and her father lived in a variety of settlements around San Diego. She eventually settled in Lemon Grove with her husband, Pepe Lieras, another native of San José del Cabo.

Pepe Lieras had arrived in San Diego after Antonia Nuñez. He had spent his early years in San José del Cabo, where he had known a number of families whose members also came to San Diego. Among these families were los Alvarez and los Hollman.

The marriage of Pepe Lieras and Antonia Nuñez in 1917 was one of the early ties between Baja Californio families in San Diego. Among their earliest friends were Ramona Castellanos and Ursino Alvarez, who were both mining circuit migrants. Pepe had known Ursino's parents in San José and talked of them often in San Diego. This friendship resulted in *compadrazgo* relations as los Alvarez baptized one of the many Lieras offspring.

Los Lieras, through their offspring, provided a large base for the solidarity of the social relations among the first San Diego generation of Baja migrant families. Sra. Lieras gave birth to a total of seventeen children, of whom sixteen survived. Her offspring married into a number of Baja families. As a whole, los Lieras, parents and children, provided a series of connecting links when Lemon Grove became the geographic nexus of the network and the Californio community.

Los Hollman

The Hollman family history also reveals the patterns of mobility between the two Californias and the internal cohesion of family kin along the frontera. The Hollmans' pattern of settlement in the frontera exemplifies the seeking out of other Baja Californios, the meeting of new friends and the links formed at this time between nonkin from Baja California. The chronological outline of their migration and settlement shows constant mobility over three generations between the Californias as well as the movement between Calexico and San Diego that became a pattern for many of the early San Diego arrivals.

José Hollman originally emigrated from Berlin to South America. He then made his way to San José del Cabo, where he settled and married. His wife, Micaela Acosta, was a native San Joseña. The couple reared seven children and remained in the cape until José's death in the 1920s. Micaela then went north to San Diego where three of her offspring had migrated.

Marcos Hollman, son of José, had moved to San Diego in 1904 with his wife, Eulogia Gastelum, and two children, Bernardo and Josefa. They, like other natives of San José del Cabo, came north by steamer, disembarked in Ensenada and crossed the international line at San Ysidro. That year a daughter, Sarah, was born to the Hollmans in San Diego, but she died before the year was over. The following year Marcos went to Mexicali, while Eulogia and the children returned to San José, where they remained for about a year. They returned to San Diego again via steamer in late 1905. In 1907 they went to Calexico but crossed back into Baja California where they settled in Mexicali.

Los Hollman also illustrate the strong family networks that helped maintain a secure base for settlement along the border. Frequent visits to the south to see close kin, the arrival of close kin (maternal aunts and paternal kin), and the shared adoption of the Hollman children are obvious kin relations that fostered successful settlement in the towns of the frontera. During the next decade the Hollmans moved frequently across the border and in the peninsula. In 1910 Bernardo, the eldest son, returned to San José with a maternal aunt (who was living in San Diego) to visit his ailing grandmother. When Bernardo returned to Mexicali in 1910, revolutionary disturbances had begun to shake the town and the family crossed the border into Calexico. In 1919 both parents died, but other family members who had migrated earlier adopted the children.[5] First a maternal aunt who had married Narcisso Montejano (both natives of the cape) took the children (Bernardo, Josefa, Marcos, and Victor). Then in 1921 the children traveled to San Diego, where Josefa Gastelum de Ceseña, another maternal aunt, adopted them. Her husband, Daniel Ceseña, was also a cape native.

During these years the Hollmans also met a number of families with whom lifelong relationships were established. In Mexicali Bernardo met "Panchita," Juana, and all the Castellanos. There los Hollman also met los Salgado, another family that became incorporated into the growing Baja network. (Los Salgado are the family of my maternal

Josefa [standing], Victor, Bernardo [seated], and
Marcos Hollman, c. 1917

grandmother, Dolores Salgado de Smith.) Bernardo and his family also knew los Smith in Calexico. These acquaintances fostered formal ties that would later pull a number of families into a tight social field around the San Diego area. In Calexico Marcos and Eulogia Hollman became *compadres* to the Salgados and Bareños (from Comondú) and in San Diego to the Alvarez and Smith families. Marriages between Hollmans and Salvatierras (also from the cape) occurred in the next decades. Such interfamily ties became common in the years following the initial period of settlement.

THE SECOND STREAM:
THE TWENTIES AND THIRTIES

The second stream of Baja Californios into the frontera provided not only an increase in numbers for the network but a strengthening of the ties between families already settled. These later migrants came as part of the large influx of Mexicanos who arrived to work in the cotton industry of Mexicali. But they arrived seeking family that had settled in earlier periods of immigration. Unlike previous migrants, these late arrivals came directly north in a classic second stream. Most of the families that arrived were kin to the previous migrants. In a well-practiced pattern, they sought refuge and aid in the homes of close kin. Extended kindred, like hometown networks, continued to provide family bonds and new outlets for the growth of family interrelations.

This second stream helped to perpetuate the regional ties of migrants to the peninsula. Incoming families and friends brought news of loved ones in the south and changes among kin in the hometowns. The recent arrivals encouraged reminiscences of the bygone days that earlier settlers knew could never be recaptured.

Through marriages in the south some of the couples in the second stream had united two extended families that had also become acquainted in the north. Such marriage partners had met in gulf or interior towns through resettlement, short labor migrations, or mutual family friends. Marriages between individuals from different towns followed a pattern to that of marriages in the frontera, for when these couples went north, they often became connecting links that helped to bring two extended kindred of the migrant population together. In the case of families that were already acquainted or tied through other relations, these second-stream couples added a further link to interfamily solidarity.

When individuals came north, they were offered support by both kin and friends. Los Smith had kin living in San Diego who received them on their first arrival and provided them a place from which to survey San Diego for jobs and housing. Similarly, when Ceseñas came north, kin provided a home and adopted the young children when their parents passed away. Los Hollman, Alvarez, Becerra, and other families acted similarly. Friends often played an important role in extending support to arriving families. Los Castellanos had received los Marquez and provided a number of families with support on their arrival in San Diego.

The pattern of the second-stream migration paralleled that of the first phase of family entrance into the frontera. For this too was a family movement. In addition, the move was often prompted by the lack of economic alternatives in the hometown. The decision to leave the cape was sanctioned by existing kin in the north, and almost as a rule the migrants traveled either as nuclear families or family groups. Moreover, individuals headed directly to the border, cognizant of their destination. They knew they were going to the U.S., and this move, as a pattern, was not the slow process it had been in the case of the mining circuit migrants. This was a single move from points on the gulf to the north and the delta of the Colorado. Immigration was immediate, very often occurring within a few weeks of leaving the hometown in the south.

Unlike the previous migration, this twenties and thirties migration was part of a greater flow of Mexicanos into the developing sectors of the United States. It occurred at a time of mass immigration into the agricultural and industrial north of the United States. People were caught in the excitement of the rush north, stirred by stories of economic prosperity and employment. Steam travel was well developed by the third decade of the twentieth century, and the gulf became a highway of small vessels steaming into the northern ports of the Colorado delta to unload the *enganchados* (contracted labor; literally "the hooked") who were heading into the Mexicali and Imperial valleys of the Californias. While the majority of immigrants joined the labor circuit north into the San Joaquín Valley, the Baja Californio migrants remained along the frontera, with family and friends, within striking distance of the peninsula and hometowns in the south.

The increase in gulf travel developed as a consequence of the cotton boom in Mexicali. As the Mexicali valley grew, so too did the numbers of labor seekers who went south in search of laborers for the new economy. The small vessels that came seeking individuals to contract for cotton work in the north provided a constant travel network between the cape and the north.[6] There was at the same time movement of peninsulars across the gulf and into the mainland.

The second-stream movements and the growth of linkages in the frontera are more clearly seen in the actual stories of migrants who left their hometowns in search of better economic but similar social lifestyles. The following examples of los Bareño and los Romero illustrate the nature of the second migration and the internal patterns of relations that helped foster a network of formal social relations in the frontera.

Los Mesa–Romero and los Mesa–Bareño

In 1920 the families of Martina Mesa de Romero and her sister Berta Mesa de Bareño left the town of Loreto for the United States border. The Bareños decided to go north in search of work. Martina wanted to be with her sister, and the two discussed the possibility of seeing another sister, Apolonia Mesa de Smith, who had gone north via the mining circuit some twenty years before. Martina's reminiscence illustrates the importance of family connections in the decision to migrate: "We were doing very well in Loreto. But my sister, Berta, was coming here [the border]. She told Miguel, her husband, that she was going to come here. And I said 'I don't want to stay, I want to go with Berta, to see if we meet up with Apolonia.' We had word from Apolonia through Señor Olagos.[7] That's how we came here; with the message that Apolonia was here in Calexico."

The actual move out of Loreto was a joint family venture. Martina and her husband Olayo, their two children, along with Berta and Miguel and their six children boarded, one of the many steamers that was also taking *enganchados* to Mexicali.[8]

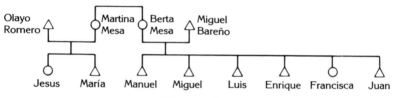

Diagram 6.
Los Mesa-Romero and los Mesa-Bareño when they left Loreto

• 112 •

Martina Mesa de Romero, San Diego, 1976

The actual move of Martina and Olayo to the north had been preceded by a series of internal migrations. Martina had been born in 1888 in San Miguel de Comondú, but after her mother died she was adopted by the Las Rosas family and sent to live in Loreto. She was later taken across the gulf to Guaymas and on to the mining boom of Cananea. In Cananea Martina met many individuals from Baja California. Her own brother Levorio had gone there earlier to work the mines and it was there that she met her husband, Olayo Romero, who was originally from Loreto.

After their marriage los Mesa-Romero lived in Cananea for two

Apolonia Mesa de Smith in San Diego, c. 1945. (Courtesy
of María Smith Alvarez)

years but moved back to Loreto where they ranched and collected *palo
blanco*[9] for about five years before deciding to accompany the Bareños
north. Their decision to leave was also influenced by an earlier migra-

tion, that of Martina's younger brother Levorio, who had gone to Mexicali as a contracted laborer in 1915. Moreover, the move north was prompted, at least for Martina, by her sister's leaving and the presence of Apolonia and Levorio in the north.

The Bareños went north for a variety of reasons, but new economic opportunities seemed to be the primary motive. Berta Mesa de Bareño and her husband Miguel had lived in Loreto. Miguel had had a variety of jobs in the region, including mailman, sheriff, and *bayuquero* (tavernkeeper). A son, Enrique, states that another reason for leaving was the revolution. The presence of Berta's sister Apolonia and her brother Levorio in the north were added inducements for migration.

The journey from Loreto to Mexicali took about a week. They boarded the steamer *La Pasita,* which stopped in Santa Rosalía, then made its way up the gulf to San Felipe. Passengers disembarked near the port of La Bomba and traveled the remaining hundred-odd miles by land to Mexicali. Once in Mexicali many families crossed directly into the United States.

Levorio Mesa was living in Mexicali when his sisters Berta and Martina arrived. Having had word from him, they found him easily. Levorio had already contacted his other sister, Apolonia Smith, in Calexico and had gone there regularly on weekends. Berta and Martina sent word to Apolonia that they had arrived and began the process of immigration immediately. The families had no trouble crossing the border and went directly to Apolonia's.

The joint migration of these two sisters and their families provided an immediate addition of kin for the Mesa extended family in the north and furthermore brought two extended lines—the Bareños and the Romeros—into the growing Calexico network. Both of these families became acquainted with other Baja Californios in Mexicali and Calexico and began to establish formal ties of their own with kin and peninsular friends.

The second-stream families became part of the northern network in a pattern similar to the development of relations among earlier migrants. Once in the north, couples produced children who were socialized along with the pioneer offspring on the border. Even the actual birth of children provided the extension of social relations. Guadalupe Salgado was a midwife and became close to many women because of this practice. In at least one instance it led to *compadrazgo* relationships. The mutual experiences of offspring in neighborhoods and schools provided another common bond between peninsulars.

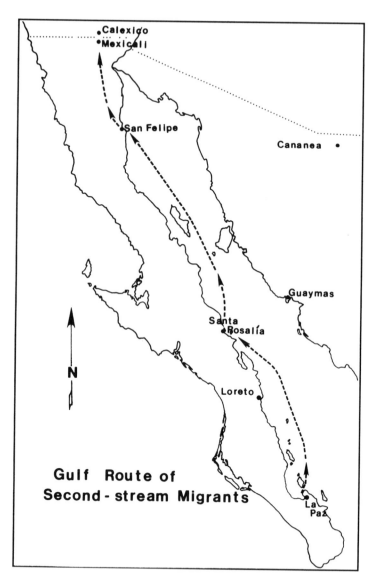

Map 7.

Close friendships were established through extended family members, and these relations often resulted in formal ties expressed in *compadrazgo* and marriage. This general pattern was a natural process of individuals' seeking out like individuals. It had occurred in the mining circuit and on the gulf and was now occurring for migrants in the frontera towns. Among both new and older migrant cohorts the normal life cycle of birth, *compadrazgo,* and marriage was given new importance by the hardships and cultural dissonance experienced in the new environment of the frontera.

– 6 –

SAN DIEGO–
LEMON GROVE:
FLORESCENCE,
1930–1950

In the summers of my youth and adolescence Lemon Grove was a special place. For that was a time of abandon, of back-porch fantasies, and of children's charades through the yards, gates, and trees of the houses that made up that little community. The "hill," an open expanse of chaparral and enticing gullies, was a territorial playground for the marauding *chamacos* (boys and girls) whose parents and grandparents had settled there. My own parents had been raised in Lemon Grove, although after their marriage they never lived there. But I went often to be with my cousins and paternal grandmother, Ramona Castellanos. The world there was an interlocked reality of neighbors and *parientes* in which we, as children, were known to be a part. Los Ceseña, Bonillas, Lieras, Alvarez, Castellanos, Nuñez, and others formed the basis of a sociocultural *ambiente* (environment) that had begun when these and other families sought each other out, settled, and perpetuated the social links that bound their community.

The arrival and early settlement of Baja Californios in the frontera region was a time of movement and family change within the county of San Diego, which at that time stretched from the Pacific to the Colorado basin. In the early years of migration there was great mobility along the international line, but eventually families that had come from the south started settling down. An era began to draw to a close as pioneer migrants gave way to a new generation of offspring that had been born and raised along the migration north as well as in the frontera towns of Calexico and San Diego. The deaths of many pioneers marked the moves of families to San Diego. Nonetheless, some pioneers survived longer as heads of households and remained significant in the formation of the new communities that arose in San Diego county.

The florescence of family interrelations in the town of Lemon Grove introduces a number of new concepts. These include apex families and individuals, incorporation, recurring kin connections, and the perpetuation of family ideology. Each of these concepts can be viewed as a mechanism or process that aided in the cultural development I am describing. Case studies reveal the importance of these processes, but what is less obvious is their derivation from the history, regional affiliation, migration, and settlement of families along the frontera of Alta California. The Lemon Grove phase forms a part of the whole migration process and network development, from the pre-Calmallí era through the frontera period. The discussion focuses on the movement of families out of Calexico and the role of job experiences, kin ties, and family support in migration. I stress here the individual perceptions and behavior of migrants in an effort to document personal histories and present the combined factors that influenced migration and settlement.

CALEXICO TO SAN DIEGO

Baja Californio migration along the frontera between San Diego and Calexico began in the first decade of the twentieth century and included migrant movement across the border to the homes of siblings and other kin living in Mexicali, Tijuana, Ensenada, and Tecate. Migration in the early 1920s was characterized by a mobility unmatched in previous or later periods. Hometown visits and visits from southerly kin were common at this time, and the social and kin linkages between individuals and families on both sides of the border became increasingly vivid. These ties encouraged moves from Calexico to the city of San Diego.

Families and individuals migrated principally for economic reasons, but family sanctions in these moves were often equally important. Family communications about the travels and experiences of other Baja Californios and about opportunities for employment in San Diego county enticed other migrants to relocate. Most of the migrants who had worked in Calexico were dissatisfied with their work and the style of life there in general. This dissatisfaction resulted when migrants compared jobs they had held along the mining circuit or in the *am-*

biente of the southern hometowns with jobs in Calexico, where most worked at unskilled labor.

Manuel Smith: Kin Ties and Support

Manuel Smith (my great-grandfather) arrived in Calexico from the mining circuit, where he had been an independent *leñador*. But in Calexico he worked odd jobs and became dependent on the agricultural cycle. In the mining towns he had owned his own mules and collected wood to sell for use in the smelters. In Calexico he picked crops primarily on private ranches. As time passed, Manuel became increasingly disenchanted with the available work and the lack of other possibilities in Calexico and decided to scout the San Diego area for better prospects. Manuel and his son Adalberto traveled to San Diego in a horse-drawn wagon across the Laguna Mountains. In El Cajon they were received by Malvino Smith, a paternal uncle of Manuel's and the son of Antonio Smith, who had left Comondú with Manuel over twenty years before. There they saw rich ranches, the developing city of San Diego, and numerous Baja Californios who had settled the area. They returned to Calexico with plans to move to the San Diego area.

Back in Calexico they gathered their families and as an extended kin group began the trek to San Diego. Three nuclear families joined in the move: Manuel and Apolonia and two unmarried sons; Adalberto (the eldest), his wife, Dolores Salgado, and their children; and Berta Mesa de Bareño, Apolonia's sister, and her family. Los Smith went first to Fresno to earn money for later settlement and remained there,

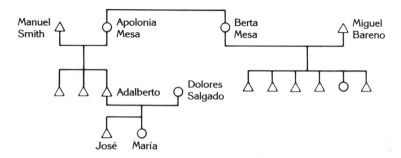

Diagram 7.
Los Mesa-Smith and los Bareño when they left Calexico
for San Diego, c. 1925

Adalberto Smith and Dolores Salgado, Calexico, c. 1918

picking fruit, for about a year. Then with the earned money they moved south to their ultimate destination and settled in Lemon Grove.

Olayo Romero: Kin and Jobs

Kin were important not only in communicating and offering support to migrants seeking work in San Diego, but in facilitating direct job contacts. In 1925 Olayo Romero and his brother-in-law Levorio Mesa (brother of Apolonia Mesa de Smith, Martina Mesa de Romero, and Berta Mesa de Bareño) went to San Diego to look for work that would allow them to leave Calexico. Olayo had been picking cotton in Calexico and supplementing his income with construction work. Like other migrants he too was unhappy. Olayo left his wife and family in Calexico, unsure of the job possibilities in San Diego. But when he and Levorio arrived in San Diego they met a cousin of Martina and Levorio who gave them a job. Martina reported: "Olayo worked in Lemon Grove. Haven't you seen that rock quarry that's over there? Olayo worked there. My brother Levorio and Olayo came first. I stayed in Calexico. The man who was the manager at the quarry, the *mayordomo*, was

Diagram 8.
Los Mesa and los Romero

Faracisco Espinosa, a first cousin of mine. And he gave them work."
This work allowed Olayo to send for his wife, Martina, and settle in San Diego.

The kin support that was an important factor in the successful moves of los Romero, los Mesa, and los Smith to San Diego came in a variety of ways. In the case of los Romero, kin were directly responsible for securing jobs for the new arrivals. But for los Smith, kin provided more general support in the search for housing and employment. Kin support came in yet another manner to other migrants: adoption and sibling support. The number of offspring in migrant families was generally large and as heads of households aged and died, some left children too young to survive on their own. The strong family cohesion fostered by the institutions of kin extension and kin support provided secure "homes" for these youth. Many children were adopted by older siblings, by aunts and uncles, or by other kin who had settled in San Diego. This problem of orphans signaled the end of an era.

As the era of the first generation of pioneer migrants was coming to a close, a new generation of offspring, born in migration and in the early settlement periods, became increasingly important. A natural unfolding of a new cohort group that had been raised in the frontera took place during this period.

Los Castellanos and los Sotelo: Adoption and Life-cycle Transition

In addition to illustrating adoption as a principal mechanism in migration, the following cases show how kin and friendship ties on both sides of the border provided support for migrants. Los Castellanos had close family living in Mexicali and Tijuana, and los Sotelo moved directly from Mexicali to San Diego through similar support. In both these cases the life cycle and the transition of a new migrant cohort group into family leadership is a continuous theme.

The children of Narcisso and Cleofas Castellanos left the Calexico

The family of Adalberto Smith in Mexicali visiting the Salgados in 1924, just before leaving for San Diego. Standing in rear (left to right): Guadalupe Salgado and Dolores Salgado de Smith. Adalberto sits holding José with María standing. (Courtesy of María Smith Alvarez)

Adalberto Smith with his two children, María and José, in
Mexicali, 1924. (Courtesy of María Smith Alvarez)

region when both their parents died (Narcisso in Mexicali in 1918 and
Cleofas two years later). They were survived by five unmarried children
who had been raised on the frontera and by three married offspring
living in the West Coast towns of Ensenada, Tijuana, and San Diego.
The family decided that the remaining children should reside in San

Diego with Ramona Castellanos, their eldest sister, and her husband, Ursino Alvarez.

The children left Mexicali through the assistance of Abel (a brother who had married Maria Moore of San Diego), who was working in Tijuana as a chauffeur on the route from San Diego to Tijuana. Abel sent a car to pick up his younger siblings in Mexicali and he met them in Tijuana. Ursino Alvarez also came to Tijuana to lead the children across the border to his and Ramona's house in La Mesa, a small community on San Diego's outskirts. The children remained with Ramona until each of them married. Through her family leadership role, Ramona, as eldest, became the acting head of los Castellanos. She reared her younger siblings and her own children while becoming a principal figure in the Baja Californio network in San Diego.

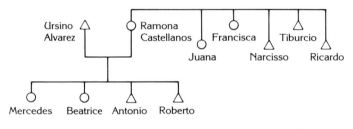

Diagram 9.
Los Castellanos and los Alvarez in La Mesa, 1920

Los Sotelo were similarly affected by the loss of one of their parents, but rather than receiving support directly from close kin, they were aided by close migrant friends (who are now recognized as distant relatives by Sotelo descendants). Their case illustrates the kinlike support between migrant families which later aided in the development of a tight network of kin.

Don Pancho and Angelina Sotelo arrived in Calexico in 1914. Don Pancho worked in Mexicali, where the family had settled. But when Angelina passed away in 1921, Don Pancho decided to move west. In San Diego, los Sotelo had numerous friends from the mining circuit and from Calexico as well. Los Castellanos, who had been close friends since Las Flores, and los Simpson, friends from Calmallí times, were living in San Diego. When Francisco and the children arrived in San Diego, Guillermo and Artemicia Simpson gave them lodging and support. They stayed with los Simpson until Francisco found housing in Lemon Grove, where he then settled down.

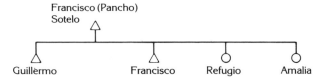

Diagram 10.
Los Sotelo when they left Calexico-Mexicali
for San Diego, c. 1920

These examples help illustrate the similarity of the Calexico-San Diego move to the moves made by migrants along the mining circuit, on early steamers, and in the second-stream migration. Individuals traveled as family and kin groups. They went to areas where kin and friends received and offered them aid and security while they looked for jobs and secured housing. As in previous migratory periods, the prospects of better employment, for those seeking work, was sanctioned by the presence and support of family and friends in the new towns. For those individuals who were forced to leave Calexico and Mexicali to seek support, it was close family and friends in San Diego who provided that security.

THE FRONTERA TOWNS:
GEOGRAPHIC AND FAMILY CONNECTIONS

Settlement of Baja Californios during the early decades of the twentieth century was not limited to San Diego. Families also settled in Mexicali, Calexico, and Tijuana. Some family members also moved farther south, to Ensenada, another concentration of population.

On the Mexican side Mexicali and Tijuana experienced the most dramatic development and attracted many more settlers than did Ensenada to the south. Counterparts of the U.S. cities of San Diego and Calexico, these Mexican towns also began developing rapidly. Mexicali took on a character of its own as the Mexicali valley grew, and Tijuana developed in response to the dynamic American city across the border.

The settlers of the northern peninsular border towns maintained close familial ties and relationships with family members and friends in the United States. Some of these individuals eventually settled permanently in San Diego, although many other individuals reentered Mexico to settle at later periods.

The settlement of individuals from the same immediate families, other kin, and friends along both sides of the border perpetuated cross-border movement similar to the unrestricted crossings that had been prominent in the early part of the century. San Diego settlers went to Ensenada, Tecate, Tijuana, and Mexicali to visit siblings and other close kin settled in these towns. And for new migrants seeking entrance into the United States the homes of kin in the Mexican border towns were stopping points where newcomers obtained information and communicated with kin across the border. This pattern of communication, travel, and maintenance of kin ties along the border became more pronounced in the 1930s as Lemon Grove and San Diego became recognized communities of Baja Californios.

Lemon Grove

Lemon Grove, like the other towns singled out in this study, represents a specific time and setting that was important in shaping the settlement and interactions of the families of this study. Although families were settling in a variety of locales in and around San Diego, a nucleus of people settled in Lemon Grove. This nucleus represented the majority of migrant families, including individuals from all phases of migration and with regional ties that kept the Baja Californios together. In the small community of Lemon Grove mining circuit migrants and early steamer and second-stream individuals came together, often fusing several branches of Baja families into a large sociocultural network. Day-to-day contacts between pioneer migrants, migrant offspring, and the new border generation were continual reinforcements of the network's ideological and sociocultural bonds with hometowns, kin in the south, and the peninsula as a whole.

People came to Lemon Grove for a number of economic reasons. Lemon Grove was a small rural community, yet it offered a variety of employment possibilities. The community of Mexicanos was situated in a valley floor surrounded by large citrus orchards and a variety of agricultural fields. The orchards and a packinghouse provided immediate work for most incoming migrants. A railroad, also a job incentive, passed through the community and was the main means of

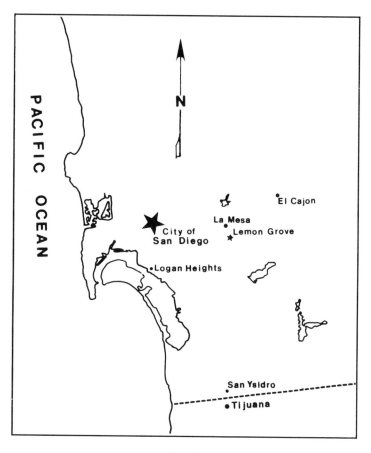

Map 8.
San Diego County

transport for produce out of the town. Along with these potential em-
ployers, a nearby rock quarry employed numerous Baja Californios as
miners and laborers. Furthermore, Lemon Grove was only ten miles
from San Diego, where there were a variety of opportunities in construction and general labor.

In a real sense Lemon Grove resembled the towns from which
migrants had come. It was a self-contained sociocultural community
that provided security in the form of available jobs and sociocultural
support from kin and friends who had settled and were settling there.

Adalberto Smith in Lemon Grove, 1926

Important life events were shared by the community as a whole, and other kin and friends lived nearby in San Diego and eastward in El Cajon.

Individuals and families who left Calexico and arrived in San Diego and Lemon Grove were received by a number of individuals who had arrived here earlier. Many of these individuals were early steamer and mining circuit migrants. Los Lieras, los Nuñez, los Alvarez, los Castellanos, los Ceseña, los Guilin, and other families had settled in San Diego and were living in Lemon Grove. Abel Alvarez had wed Ramona de las Rosas, originally from San José del Cabo, and settled here. Nicolás Ceseña came to Lemon Grove with his wife, Luisa Chavez, and son. Ramona Castellanos de Alvarez settled here with her own offspring and a number of siblings. Los Gonzales, Smith, Sotelo, Mesa, and a

Dolores Salgado de Smith with her two children, María and José,
in Lemon Grove, 1926. (Courtesy of María Smith Alvarez)

host of other families came to settle in the little community and raise
their families.

Many migrants were attracted to Lemon Grove but found life in
the United States far from perfect; as a result, many early settlers
decided to return to the peninsula. As always, these return moves
fostered the kin and geographic affiliation of Baja families throughout
the frontera zone. Most of the returnees did not go back to their
hometowns of the cape but chose to remain in the frontera near family.
Juana Castellanos married in San Diego but she and her husband

settled in Tijuana. Her brothers Abel and Jesus were already living in the northern peninsula with spouses they had wed in the United States. Los Mesa, Sotelo, and Mesa-Smith all have relatives living in the frontera towns of Baja California. Most of these people tried living in the United States but for a variety of reasons chose to live in Baja California. During the 1930s Hirginia Mesa de Ceseña crossed to San Diego but remained less than a year. She says, "Era muy duro" (It was very hard). The work there was not good and she did not want her husband to work so hard for so little. "Que anda uno robando allá, en tierras ajenas?" (Why should a person steal his living in foreign lands?) Her parents had also crossed but returned to live in Baja too. Her sister Paula went to the United States about 1924 with her husband, Ramon Espinoza, who had siblings and parents in San Diego. They went to Santa Ana, then returned to Tijuana, then reentered the United States to live in Santee, Lakeside, and finally Lemon Grove. They remained a total of four years but ultimately returned because Paula's parents were in Ensenada and the family had all become ill in the United States. They settled in Maneadero, near Ensenada, then in the 1950s moved to Tecate.

Many of the individuals who returned to Baja were pioneer migrants or elder children of the first migrant groups. Older individuals who had continually been disenchanted with jobs and cultural dissonance returned in their later years to be "in Mexico" and on the peninsula. Francisco Becerra returned to live near Ensenada, where he had purchased a ranch. Widowed wives also returned and lived with offspring across the line. In many cases elderly individuals insisted on living in Mexico, fostering movement of offspring into the town of Tijuana.

Lemon Grove represents a phase in which the extension of kin among related and unrelated families reached a peak. In the previous phases, in Calmallí and Calexico, friends and families had come together. They had raised their children, extended *compadrazgos,* and intermarried, but in San Diego and especially in Lemon Grove these interrelations served as a basis for multiple kinship bonds between families. The network not only grew in numbers but took on a qualitative density previously unmatched. *Compadrazgos* and marriages increased between families, and several new branches of extended kin were incorporated into the network of relations. Multiple *compadrazgos* and marriages between the specific set of families provided a multiplication of family bonds and identification recognized by all members.

Everyone was related. They all shared day-to-day experiences, and sociocultural events reaffirmed the identity, *parentesco,* mutual support, and historical relations of the community.

Migrants were not the sole participants in the formation of close relations, for their children played a significant role in the network development. This cohort shared a number of experiences that helped to solidify their relations as a group. Many attended school together and passed through adolescence as a cohort group. Children were often together at social gatherings of family and community and developed close ties with their own age mates. They were often closely related and their families shared close ties in the community and in work. A strong web of relations bound the community together.

Lemon Grove was the setting, but as in the past, the community was defined by the rich social relations that fostered communal types of bonds and kept migrants together. Despite difficult and sometimes severe socioeconomic and geographic constraints, social relations based on traditional institutions (expressed in new configurations) were the permeating factors that allowed individual expression and the growth of strong ties.

THE PROCESSES AND MECHANISMS OF NETWORK FORMATION

The family interrelations that led to a formal network of kin ties in San Diego are best illustrated by the mechanisms that aided in establishing these relations. A variety of social kin linkages helped produce solidarity between families from Baja California. These linkages are interdependent cogs in a larger sociocultural process that as a systematic whole produced an interconnected web of kin relations. The linkages occurred throughout migration and settlement, but it was only in the frontera that they brought together a number of extended families that otherwise would not have been part of this network.

A number of kin and kinlike linkages fostered by particular families and individuals brought unrelated participants together and promoted the development of kin institutions between families (especially in the case of nonkin). I refer to these particular families as apex individuals and families because of their role in linking the network at various stages of growth. The institutions of *compadrazgo, parentesco,* and marriage were the final stages of the linkages in which ties were actually formalized.

Apex Families

Apex families helped develop a formal base of kin ties between previously related and unrelated families. These were important links that brought together the social fields of separate families, primarily through marriage and *compadrazgo*. These key families first provided a linkage for reciprocity between both settled and arriving migrants. Their own migration experience had introduced them to new families and friends. They became a common link between their own kin and new friends and between their various groups of new friends.

The common cultural and historic background of migrants was the initial base on which the extension of friendship and kin ties was built and deemed socially acceptable. This may seem obvious, but the regional particulars of Baja migrants' backgrounds have specific importance in the development of this network. In addition to *Mexicanidad*[1] and common language, apex families and those they brought together shared a recognized history associated with the peninsula. They shared mutual relations with a number of nonrelated Baja families and brought about face-to-face contact and reciprocity between such families. Reciprocity and friendship eventually led to formal ties of kinship and an extension of the Baja Californio network.[2]

The family of los Simpson illustrates the apex linkage in the maze of closely related families I am describing. This apex linkage was fostered by premigration kin ties, migration friendships, multiple reciprocity and aid offered to friends and relations in the border region.

Los Simpson. The ties of los Simpson with other frontera settlers began in the cape pueblo of San Antonio and developed through the family's migration north. In San Antonio los Simpson knew the family of Loreto Marquez (to whom, descendants state, they were distantly related) before los Marquez went north to Las Flores around 1890.[3] The Simpsons also went on the mining circuit, where they met and united with other families that became part of the network. In Calmallí they met los Castellanos, Sotelo, Smith, Bolume, and others. Los Simpson eventually went to San Fernando, then crossed the border at Campo and headed east to Calexico.

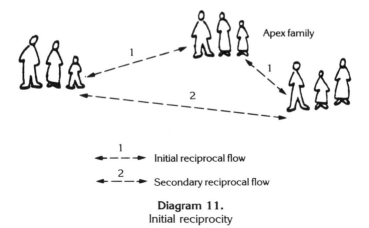

Diagram 11.
Initial reciprocity

The Simpsons' assistance to families entering the frontera shows the mutual aid and kinlike support they extended to other mining families. In Calexico they offered their home and assistance to the family of Don Pancho Sotelo until the new arrivals found work in Mexicali and moved across the border. In the same period Narcisso Castellanos, his wife Cleofas, and their children stayed with Guillermo and Artemicia Simpson until they too found work. The mutual friendships of the mining circuit experience were further enhanced not solely by the assistance and support offered by the Simpsons but also through the social sentiment and solidarity of mutual friendship between these families.

In a pattern now familiar the Simpsons left Calexico, traveled west, and settled in San Diego. There, once again, they received Pancho Sotelo and his family, who had left Calexico and now sought help in settling in San Diego. The Sotelos remained in the Simpson household until Don Pancho got a job and moved to Lemon Grove.

The kin linkages of the Simpsons are also illustrative of their apex role in the tight web of interrelations among the Baja Californio population. Los Sotelo speak about their kin relation to los Simpson. Descendants speak of this as a distant tie that became significant after migration. *Confianza* and friendships derived from the migration experience appear to be the important link that established close ties between the two families. Los Sotelo are related to los Simpson through Señora Artemicia Simpson (whom Guillermo met and wed in San Ignacio). Don Francisco's wife Angelina was Sra. Artemicia's maternal

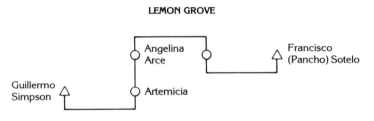

Diagram 12.
The kin ties of los Simpson and los Sotelo

aunt. These links were further strengthened among second-generation frontera offspring. The close friendships of the Sotelos and Castellanos provided a base for the marriage between offspring of these families. Refugio Sotelo and Tiburcio Castellanos were wed in San Diego, and when Guillermo Simpson's son (Guillermo II) married and had children, los Castellanos served as *padrinos de bautismo* (baptismal godparents), forming a *compadrazgo* relationship between these families. The linkage does not stop here. Guillermo Simpson (II) married Sarah Fernandez, whose family had come north from Santa Rosalía during

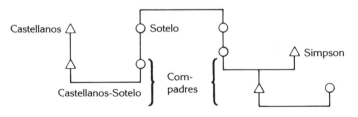

Diagram 13.
The *compadrazgo* relationship between los
Castellanos-Sotelo and los Simpson

the mining circuit period. This link united another network of families that had become acquainted on the mining circuit but had not become formally linked. Sarah Fernandez's sister Flora married Manuel Smith II, son of Apolonia Mesa and Manuel Smith from Comondú. Furthermore, the Fernandez family can be traced directly to the Mesas of Comondú, who are direct descendants of Apolonia Mesa-Smith.

The *compadrazgo* relationships between the Simpsons and the Castellanos-Sotelos, along with the marriage of Guillermo Simpson to Flora Fernandez, brought two extended families together into a web of relations. This network was further cemented by a series of *compadraz-*

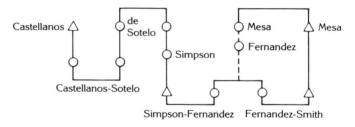

Diagram 14.
The Simpson linkage to Castellanos-Sotelo and Fernandez-Smith

gos and marriages. The most obvious and important is the second marriage of Don Francisco Sotelo himself. Don Francisco married Sarah Fernandez de Simpson's maternal aunt (Refugio) in the late 1920s (see diagram 15).

This complicated set of linkages illustrates the multiple sets of interfamily relations in Calexico and San Diego during the 1920s. This example is only a skeletal outline of the matrix of interpersonal relations between kin and nonkin in the frontera region which produced social fields among these families. The Simpsons, like other apex families, provided key links in marriages and *compadrazgos* which helped form a tight social community in San Diego during the 1930s.

Apex families and individuals play a role similar to that of centralizing women (see the history of the Gomez family in Lomnitz 1978). Like centralizing women, apex families provided emotional centrality and leadership for a variety of network members. This emotional sharing was based primarily on mutual experiences, *confianza, parentesco,* and the recognition of a similar sociocultural standing (class). This sentiment was further emphasized in the mutual aid and reciprocity of relations and extension of kinship between network members. Unlike the patron-client relationships discussed by Lomnitz, the role of apex families remains at the level of mutual aid; there are no "big men" of upper class and better economic standing who, because of class standing, become apex individuals. During frontera era settlement in San Diego, the network was a homogeneous class composed of laborers and small entrepreneurs. Indeed, economic aid and reciprocity was an important component of network development, but shared experiences, kin ties, and acquaintances that fostered *parentesco* and the mutual responsibility such sentiment requires were of prime importance. Apex families, like apex individuals, are also differentiated from

1928   1978

The Children and Grandchildren
of
Mr. and Mrs. Tom G. Castellanos
request the pleasure of your company
in honour of their parents
Fiftieth Wedding Anniversary
Saturday, September sixteenth,
nineteen hundred and seventy-eight

Knights of Columbus
4425 Home Avenue
San Diego, California

Reception - 8:00 p.m.-9 p.m.
Dance - 9:00 p.m.-1:00 a.m.   "Invitation Only"

**Family Invitation to Fiftieth Wedding Anniversary of
Refugio Sotelo and Tiburcio Castellanos**

centralizing personalities because they aid in the formation of key kin linkages between a variety of families. The Simpsons clearly illustrate such linkages through various generations and members of their family.

Apex Individuals

Apex individuals are key individuals who, through their own marriages, *compadrazgo* ties, and experiences created specific network linkages within a large set of families.

Refugio Gonzales de Sotelo. Refugio Gonzales was born in 1888 in San José de Magdalena, a small town near Santa Rosalía, but after marriage she traveled north and eventually settled in Lemon Grove. Refugio was a direct descendant of the Mesas of Comondú, but she was raised primarily in Santa Rosalía, where her father worked in the mines of El Boleo. In 1916 she married Albino Vargas, a captain of small boats who commuted between various gulf ports, and the couple went to live in Guaymas, across the gulf. In the next decade she and her immediate family moved north to Nogales, where her husband died. She then crossed the border with her children and traveled first to Los Angeles, where she remained with her mother-in-law until 1928; then she moved south to Lemon Grove.

Refugio came to Lemon Grove because her parents (who had arrived in 1926 from Cananea) and a sister, Balvina Fernandez, were there. Balvina had married Antonio Fernandez (before Refugio married) and traveled north through the mining circuit to San Diego.

When Refugio came to Lemon Grove, she met a variety of other Baja Californios. Among the families and individuals she met was Francisco Sotelo, whom she married one year later, establishing a network tie between two family extensions that had been acquainted in the migration north as well as in Lemon Grove. The Sotelos were part of the network that included los Castellanos, Alvarez, Simpson, and other closely related families. Refugio's marriage formally served to link this network with the Mesa-Smiths. Although these families had known each other from other settlement periods, this linkage, like others between these family groups, helped formalize the previous acquaintances and interrelationships. The close ties of the Sotelo-Castellanos become evident in the marriages of Francisco Sotelo's daughters into the Castellanos family.

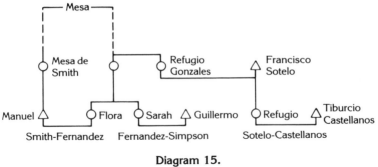

Diagram 15.
The linkage of Mesa-Smiths to Sotelo-Castellanos

Refugio Sotelo's linkage of the families also came through *com-padrazgo* relations as well as through marriage. Tiburcio Castellanos and his niece Mercedes baptized Refugio's first son. This example illustrates only a fraction of the interconnections between these families.

Guadalupe Bolume. Guadalupe Bolume is a central figure in the creation of qualitative and dense relationships between Baja Californio families. Her experience in the mining circuit became a base for the extension of kin relations in her own marriage to a mining circuit migrant as well as in marriages between her own offspring and other Baja Californios who settled in San Diego. Her offspring married into families of original Baja pioneer migrants. Diagram 16 illustrates her central position, through her offspring, in formally bringing together these families. These marriages formally linking families were more than just expressions of solidarity between Baja migrants. The individuals of these families were close friends and were proud of the sentiment they shared. Romances and weddings developed from their closeness as did *compadrazgos*. Formal ties became ways to express close sentiment and relations between individuals and families. Such ties not only brought individuals together but they also formalized and ritualized social interactions in a number of social and cultural events practiced by these families. Baptisms, marriages, birthday celebrations, funerals, and U.S. and Mexican holidays alike became large network social events of kin whose roots lay in Baja California and the migration trail.

Apex individuals, then, like apex families, were not solely bringing together migrant families through marriage and *compadrazgo*. As

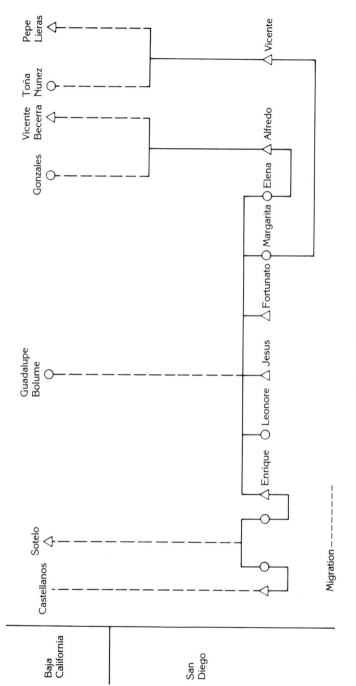

Diagram 16.

Marriage ties of Guadalupe Bolume's offspring showing network linkages and family origin in migration

central figures in the network they helped produce continuing ties that had begun in the migration process. These respected individuals continue to be recognized catalysts among the community of Baja families in San Diego.

The tight web of relations fostered by marriages between families was further intensified by the incorporation of non-Baja Californio families into the network. This took place in Calexico as well as in San Diego, but it was in Lemon Grove that such incorporation took on a specific role in maintaining interrelations of the Baja Californio community.

Incorporation

As Baja Californios crossed the border and settled in San Diego, other Mexicanos arrived and became part of the migrant community. Immigration from mainland Mexico had diminished after the turn of the century compared to the influx of mainlanders who had come in the decades of the revolution, when transportation was developing in the northern sections of the mainland. Nonetheless, some individuals and families continued to arrive and settle in San Diego. The sparse immigrant population congregated in a variety of neighborhoods, but Lemon Grove was the most prominent settling place. Some of these mainland families became incorporated into the network of Baja Californios.

Incorporation can be defined as the recruitment of (in this case, mainland) families which promoted boundary maintenance and internal cohesion of the Baja Californio network. The term *recruitment* is used loosely here, for Baja Californios did not actively seek out new families. Incorporation occurred as a natural process among individuals who shared a common language and culture. The absorption of new families served to pull specific families into the network and helped to solidify and intensify interrelations among Baja Californios.

Incorporated families united various Baja California families. Marriages between members of mainland families and individuals from a variety of Baja families created overlapping kindreds bringing Baja Californios together in formal kin connections. This is best illustrated through genealogical examples of intermarriages. The cases of los Bonilla and los Oyos are two such examples. Both the Bonilla and Oyos families came directly from the Mexican mainland and settled in Lemon Grove, where they met and shared daily experiences with the other members of that community.

Los Bonilla.   Los Bonilla provided a base for a number of linkages between families settled in Lemon Grove. Los Bonilla were among the first families in Lemon Grove, settling there during the early decades of the century, before it became a Mexicano community. They lived within a quarter-mile radius of numerous Alvarez, Ceseña, Castellanos, Guilin, Sotelo, and Lieras family members who made up the basis of the network. Nine women were born to the Bonillas and were raised and socialized with Baja Californios and other Mexicanos.

The marriages of the Bonilla children reveal the close ties this family maintained with Baja Californios as well as the strengthened ties that developed between Baja Californios as a result of these marriages. Marriages between Bonillas and Castellanos, Bonillas and Ceseñas, Bonillas and Alvarezes, Bonillas and Gonzales-Nuñezes served to unite these families in formal relationships. Diagram 17 charts these marriage ties and the origins of intermarrying family. The immediate result

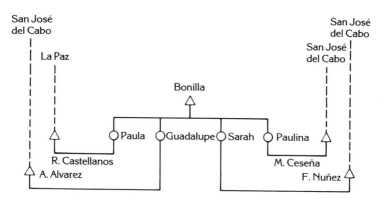

Diagram 17.
Bonilla marriage ties and origins of spouses' families

of such ties was the creation of formal affinal bonds between all these families and the development of a large kindred of interrelated Baja families of which offspring were members. Additional marriages reemphasized these ties. Alvarez married Smith (Comondú), Castellanos married Sotelo. These ties help to illustrate a complex set of interfamily relations that were in part created through incorporation. In addition to marriage ties, *compadrazgo* between these families was similarly multiple.

Incorporation can also be distinguished in later generations. The

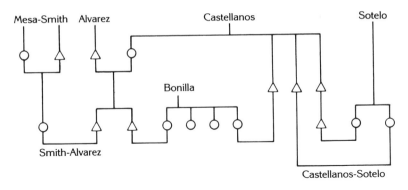

Diagram 18.
Continuing marriages of network offspring

marriages between los Oyos and los Sotelo-Castellanos is one such example that illustrates the maintenance of family solidarity and intra-family relations.

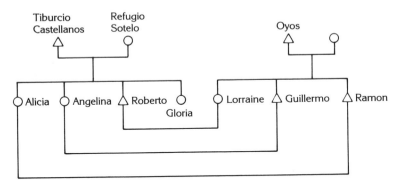

Diagram 19.
Castellanos-Oyos ties

Certainly such ties were not planned; nor was the sole purpose of these marriages to maintain tight family bonds within and between familia from Baja California. Los Oyos, los Bonilla, and other families had become close, respected friends who shared and contributed to the establishment of a strong sociocultural community of Mexicanos in San Diego.

The mechanisms I have discussed thus far were significant components in the formation of a strong network of kin relations among the families of this study. The apex families and individuals served to formally unite not only dyads (in the form of families) but myriads of families who were already familiar and shared bonds. Incorporation was equally important as a middle-ground process, bringing together a wide set of families who shared regional background, migration, and settlement. A similar mechanism is the tie between families resulting from recurring kin connections.

Recurring Kin Connections

The processes I have been describing are manifest in a specific pattern of recurring kin connections which becomes evident when viewed over several generations. Recurring kin connections, along with the other kin processes and the mechanisms of incorporation and apex families, aid in the identification of a true sociocultural pattern. Viewed in this way, the network is not solely an arbitrary set of relations that brings together a group of families with similar histories. It is a sociocultural pattern identified by a specific history, specific institutions, and shared sociocultural behavior.

Recurring kin connections are specific kin ties that developed in Baja California and recurred after the families' migration to the frontera zone. Such ties are best viewed in marriage ties between families over several generations and are evident between descendants who intermarried in the U.S. a half century and as much as a century later. When viewed in relation to the migration experience, these recurring ties encompass a field of border families that previously shared relations or were closely linked through extended or affinal kin ties. Ties of this sort not only united two family branches but they helped sustain and reinforce kin and social relations while creating new bonds based on contemporary sentiment and mutual support. The resulting pattern of linkages help create and solidify the community in San Diego (see diagram 20).

Family ties in San Diego in the early twentieth century intensified for a number of reasons, for extensions of kin relationships coincided with a dramatic period of change. New social forces were shaping international attitudes and U.S. and Mexican government relationships as well as the face-to-face relations of immigrants and natives who settled in the border zone.

The impact of the border environment, especially for those who settled in the U.S., was a major force intensifying the mutual help and kin ties that led to a discernible family network. Across the border in the nearby towns of Tijuana, Tecate, Mexicali, and Ensenada, no similar definable network developed. Early migrant pioneers from the south did intermarry, but once the Baja families settled in the northern peninsula they began to intermarry with other Mexicanos from the mainland. During this period Tijuana and Mexicali were propelled into the limelight as urban nuclei and receiving zones for one of the greatest migrations in Mexican history.

The families that returned to the peninsula and those that had remained in the Mexican border towns did not share the need to perpetuate a sociocultural identity because they were not threatened by a foreign culture. They settled in Mexican towns, intermarried with Mexicans in a natural fashion, and extended kin institutions among other northern settlers. In San Diego, however, individuals were in a non-Mexican environment and had to seek out other Mexicanos and in this case trusted kin and acquaintances to be assured of successful sociocultural survival. The relationship of experience, mutual kin, regional ties, and history surfaced as a common ground for mutual aid and support in a precarious environment. Numerous family departures from the United States bear witness to the problems of cultural dissonance as do the marriage partners chosen among San Diego families. Among los Sotelo, the two children who remained with Don Pancho in Lemon Grove married into a Baja California family that had been their persistent companion from the days of the mining circuit (los Castellanos). The other four children who were not in Lemon Grove married Mexicanos from the mainland. Two had remained in Mexico before marrying, the third had gone to live in Tijuana before marrying, and the fourth individual had traveled north to San Pedro where he also married a mainland Mexicana. The history of other families reveals similar examples. More evidence is manifest in the marriages of pioneer migrant offspring who returned to Mexico. In these cases marriage to native Baja Californios was rare. Communities in Mexico were and are settlements of regionally integrated Mexicanos.

My purpose here is not to prove the uniqueness of Baja Californios in the United States but to show how these people used Mexicano family institutions within new and threatening sociocultural circumstances. The creative adaptability of these institutions and people allowed sociocultural survival and long-range cultural maintenance. Like

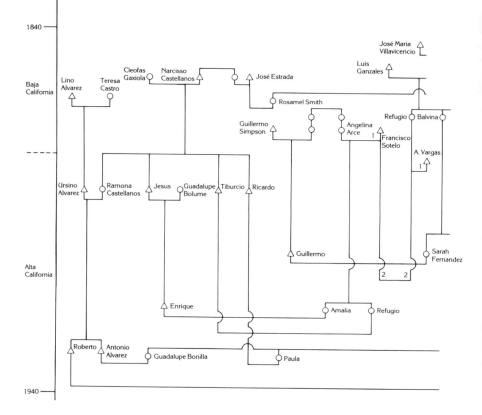

Diagram 20.
Prominent examples of recurring kin connections in the family
network, 1840–1940

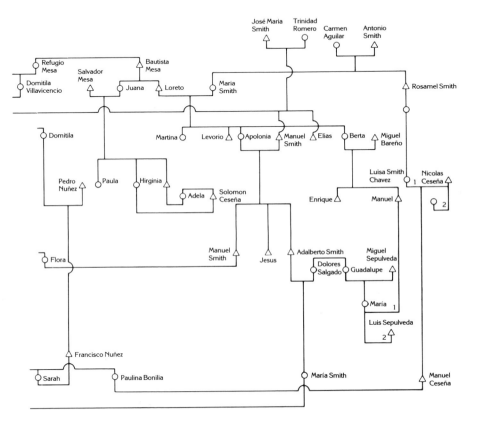

other migrant communities, Baja Californios illustrate the propensity and flexibility of cultural institutions to preserve and create new patterns without creating social disequilibrium.

Family Ideology

Regional ties, hometown sentiment, and the relationships based on such geographic bases all contribute to a body of ideas shared by Baja California migrants. This body of ideas as an ideology is specific to individuals and families who arrived and settled along the frontera during and after the turn of the century. As a manifestation of the regional ties and experiences shared by Baja Californios the ethos was internalized and became a mechanism and promoted the development of the network. This ideology is identified and expressed in both communication and behavior and is perhaps the strongest identifiable sentiment that had been expressed by pioneers and their offspring. People speak of the peninsula in terms of the early individuals who passed through specific geographic areas and in terms of hometowns, friends, and kin. Los Smith, los McLish, los Simpson, los Green are names important in lore particular to the peninsula and elicit tales of peninsular history, early settlement in San Diego, and continuing ties with the peninsula. Tales and manifestations of kin meeting kin, of travels in the peninsula, of hardships, and of nationality combine to form an ideology that stems not only from the main Mexican cultural background of Baja Californios but from the shared experiences of migration and settlement. The ideology, in part, strengthens ties to the peninsula but at the same time is unique in strengthening intrafamily recognition and identity. Ideology is expressed in a variety of ways. It is expressed in patriotism to Mexico, in nationality, in the choice to have children born on the peninsula, and in family lore.

Mexican nationality and patriotism is perhaps the clearest early manifestation of this ideology. Many pioneer migrants, although settled and working in the United States, maintained strong sentiment for the peninsula. This can be viewed as *Mexicanidad,* but overall patterns and expressions by individuals indicate the importance of the peninsula in such manifestations. In one case a pioneer who had arrived in San Diego in 1907 returned to the peninsula in 1911 when an American-led group of Industrial Workers of the World invaded Baja California. He returned to defend his country against the *sin verguenzas* (shameless) Wobblies who had entered with the intention of creating an independent socialist republic. He joined the Mexican army and served as a guide in his home area. When the invasion had been repulsed, he returned to San Diego. On another occasion he returned and volunteered for the Mexican army when the United States marines landed in Vera Cruz, because, as he states, he did not want Baja California to fall into U.S. hands like Texas had.

The births of the Castellanos children can be interpreted as another ideological statement (see chapter 4). Each of Narcisso's nine children was born on the peninsula. Even after Narcisso immigrated to San Diego, he insisted that the family return for the births of the last two offspring. So in 1906 and 1908 the family returned to the mining circuit. To this day Tiburcio, who was born in Julio César, has proudly retained his citizenship, although he has spent only four years of his life in Mexico and continues to live in Lemon Grove.

Vicente Sepulveda is another example of how patriotism helped in maintaining an attachment to the peninsula. Vicente worked at the border station of Mexicali for the Mexican government, but he lived with his wife, Guadalupe Salgado, in Calexico. In 1911, when the Wobblies crossed the line to invade the peninsula, Vicente joined and fought against the *filibusteros* with the Mexican forces of Celso Vega. He was seriously wounded at the battle of Rancho de Little and taken to Mexicali, where Guadalupe met him and took him across the border into Calexico, where he died. That Vicente died in Calexico did not diminish the significance of his act, for the city was considered part of the *frontera*, regardless of the political boundary and official recognition of territoriality. From the family's perspective Vicente died defending Mexico against a group of filibustering Americans[4] from the north. Years later in the sixties Vicente's death, along with others' who died defending the peninsula, was commemorated yearly as a patriotic effort. Vicente's only daughter, Maria Sepulveda, crossed yearly from San Diego to partake in the ceremonies, keeping not only an individual's history alive but the ties of the *frontera* as well.

Family lore is intricately bound with the places and the history of the peninsula. Stories of past experiences have become important evidence of kin connections as well as romantic reminiscences of bygone days. Second and third generations recount stories of early pioneers' experiences in their hometowns and in Calmallí and Las Flores. Alfredo Becerra speaks of his father Vicente's close acquaintance with Guadalupe Bolume in Calmallí, that they had danced there together, and that Vicente had provided music (guitar) for close mining friends. In San Diego Vicente Becerra played his guitar again for Guadalupe Bolume when she wed another of his close friends, Jesus Castellanos. Nicolás Ceseña speaks of the early Californias, the entrance of the French into San José del Cabo, and the good people from the cape: "When the French arrived in San José, they found potable water and said 'Where there is a running stream there are decent human beings.'"

Baja Californios and their descendants are aware of the unique populations that arrived in the peninsula and have made this part of their lore. The tales of blue-eyed Smiths crossing the line amazing both Mexicanos and Americanos is repeated with great humor. Encounters in mid-peninsular travels with Americans produce similar tales. Manuel Smith (III) and Guillermo Simpson (III), who both return frequently to the peninsula, jokingly relate meeting a jeepload of Americans. As they approached on horseback dressed in *ranchero* fashion they introduced themselves, to the amazement of the jeep travelers. Interkin connections are also told with great relish. One story tells of a mid-peninsula traveler who is carrying mail on horseback and who meets a group of frontera Smiths. After a short period they discover that the letter carrier, the person to whom the mail is to be delivered, and the frontera individuals are all Smiths and intimately related through ancestors from Comondú. Such tales are not uncommon. Individuals speak proudly of their history, of the kinship with the peninsula and to the families that have a long history there.

This oral history constitutes an ideology that is shared and perpetuated among families and serves to help maintain group identity and solidarity. And like the other mechanisms, ideology also functions as a basis for the extension of kin and kin relations among frontera migrants and settlers, for the network is a cultural system that shares unique regional traits manifested in family institutions.

– 7 –

EPILOGUE

The network of Baja Californios who settled in San Diego county was at its height in the 1930s through the 1950s, as families coalesced in Lemon Grove. It is important to note that during the second quarter of the twentieth century these families became rooted in San Diego, and in Lemon Grove specifically. Most offspring were American citizens by birth and were members of a community that was home to them. The towns from which pioneer migrants came were still remembered, and indeed still visited from time to time, but these pueblos were no longer the bases of out-migration or kinship that fostered the development of the network in the mines or the United States. The people in Lemon Grove depended on and sought assistance from their kin, neighbors, and friends who had decided to settle in the United States.

Changes in both the immigrant community in the United States and along the border altered the nature of migration and immigration after the 1930s. Before the thirties families had traveled as groups and entered the U.S. in the footsteps of other immigrants who had followed the migration north and were in the process of settlement. These early crossings of the border were not restricted and immigration was relatively easy, but as developments along both sides of the border drew increasing numbers of people, U.S. border policy focused on immigration control. Multiple border crossings and the mobility that had been a pattern in the early period of settlement were no longer possible for newcomers. Migrants were discouraged from crossing the border and those who did entered an Anglo environment for short periods rather than as settlers. In the forties and fifties and thereafter, the Californio community in San Diego was no longer seen as a group of peninsulars but primarily as a settled U.S. community. U.S. kin continued to offer support based on kin relationships (*parentesco, compadrazgo,* and family intermarriage), but migrants no longer traveled as kin units or families. Family members continued to arrive from the south, but the majority came for short visits to the homes of kin. Some migrants recognized that U.S. kin were well acquainted with the Anglo environment and could provide help in finding jobs and housing.

During the twenties and thirties a number of sociopolitical circumstances challenged the solidarity of the network and the settlers of Lemon Grove. By the 1930s Lemon Grove had become a prosperous little community, but the depression brought economic and social constraints not only for the people of Lemon Grove but for all people of Mexican descent in the United States. The economic collapse sustained by the nation as a whole resulted in resentment against the growing Mexican population in the United States. This was particularly true in the Southwest, where the Mexican immigrant population was the largest. The basis of this sentiment was the fear that Mexicans were taking jobs from U.S. citizens and filling the welfare roles without any desire to become U.S. citizens. As the nation's economy worsened and unemployment rose, official government action reflected this reaction. National changes in immigration policy specifically aimed to curtail Mexican immigration to the United States, and a national repatriation plan was organized to alleviate the Mexican alien problem. The Hoover administration's official policy of repatriation resulted in the repatriation of over 400,000 people of Mexican descent, many of whom were U.S. citizens by birth (Balderrama 1982; Bogardus 1934; Cardoso 1974; Divine 1957; Hoffman 1974; Romo 1975; Scott 1971). In California official reports and measures heightened latent prejudices and fears concerning the growing Mexican population (Hoffman 1974; Alvarez 1986; Balderrama 1982). Media reports of alarming growth rates in the Mexican population fueled the resentment. In this atmosphere the strong maintenance of the Spanish language, values, and life-style among Mexican settlers confirmed the view that these people were a threat to the general populace. Communities such as Lemon Grove, where Mexicans congregated and lived together in "little Mexicos," became targets of public and official action.

In the late 1920s and into the 1930s schools throughout the Southwest, in Texas, Arizona, and California, began Americanization programs for immigrants (Weinberg 1977; Taylor 1928; Carter 1970).

Segregation in these schools was sanctioned under the guise of help for the immigrant. Such schools were widespread in the Los Angeles area and in the San Joaquin and Imperial Valleys of California. In Lemon Grove these actions were perceived as threats to the livelihood of the Californio network, and the Californios responded by a concerted tightening and activating the community and network.

In January 1931 the local school board in Lemon Grove attempted to segregate the children of the Mexican settlers into a specially constructed school. The PTA and the board of education met to plan the separation that would exclude the Mexican community. A two-room school was built in the heart of the Mexican community, the school board assuming that the Mexican community would docilely separate itself and send its children to the new school. The school, however, became a point of contention and the Mexican parents refused to comply with the act of segregation, relying on the bonds of solidarity that had brought them to the United States and made their settlement possible. This action clearly reveals the network as a communal organization with a goal that was not simply familial or individual, as in mutual aid for jobs and housing in the past, but communal. This was true network mobilization. When the school board took action to separate the children of Mexican descent from "American" children, the Mexican families organized a neighbors' committee and vowed to fight the school board's action. The new school, boycotted by all but one family, became known as the *caballeriza* (the barnyard). The Californio community, in a well-planned response, took their grievance to the public. Local as well as statewide Spanish and English newspapers published accounts of the segregation as well as appeals from the Lemon Grove Neighbors Committee for financial and moral support (Alvarez 1986).

Many of these parents had come north on the mining circuit or had arrived via steamer from Baja California, but most of the children had been born in the United States. The parents were incensed by the attempt at segregation and based their appeals on the U.S. citizenship of the children, the majority of whom had been born in the United States and had attended the regular school for over a decade. The parents also sought help from the Mexican counsel in San Diego (Balderrama 1982; Alvarez 1986), who took a keen interest in the case and assigned two sympathetic lawyers to defend the community. Reports in Mexican newspapers followed the case closely, and the Mexican government was in full support of the community's action.

The community filed a writ of mandate with the Superior Court of

First-generation U.S. citizens at the Lemon Grove school at the time
of the school desegregation court case, c. 1931.
(Courtesy of María Smith Alvarez)

the County of San Diego charging the school board with segregation.
In early 1931 the case was heard in San Diego. Children took the stand
to prove their knowledge of English and their general progress in
school. In March 1931 the court ruled in favor of the Mexican community of Lemon Grove and demanded the immediate reinstatement of
the children of Mexican descent in the regular school. The importance
of this case, which was the first successful court action in favor of
school desegregation in the United States, has only been recognized
recently. In addition to the legal and social ramifications this case
illustrates in dramatic form the mobilization of a group of Mexican
immigrant families. This action was clearly the outcome of network
alliance that has been conditioned over several generations of time.
The parents who formed the neighborhood organization and fought
the school board included members of the Alvarez, Castellanos, Smith,
Romero, Sotelo, Gonzales, and Simpson families among others, all of
whom had come north along the mining circuit and settled in Lemon
Grove. In addition to these families, incorporated families, now a strong

part of the community, provided additional leadership and strength in the school battle. The roster of eighty-five schoolchildren named for the school case is a list of family names whose heritage was to be found in the towns of the southern peninsula. The case itself, Roberto Alvarez v. the Lemon Grove School Board, was named after one student who represented the children at large.

In addition to this mobilization of the network in united legal action, the Californios continued to offer mutual aid and assistance to one another during these periods. The depression was hard felt everywhere, but the community survived. Work in the lemon fields continued, but wages were low and the overall hardships served to begin dispersing individuals and families, although in small numbers. Few families were repatriated, and there is only one instance of deportation during this period, an action directly linked to the school segregation case. In an attempt to apply pressure to the community one family was singled out and, on the grounds of truancy, deported in the midst of the school case. The Ruiz family had long been in Lemon Grove and the children, like the majority of the schoolchildren, had been born and raised in the U.S.

While Californios were sometimes forced to seek jobs outside of Lemon Grove, the creation of the Civilian Conservation Corps by President Roosevelt also furthered outside contact for the people of Lemon Grove. Many of the young men were recruited into the CCC and taken into service throughout the state of California. This action helped families in a number of ways. It provided a source of income (which was sent home to parents) and lessened the burden on individual households. These men were exposed to new life-styles in new areas which for some provided incentives for careers unlike those known in Lemon Grove. Nonetheless, when the depression ended, most of these individuals returned to Lemon Grove and San Diego.

The economic and social stresses in the thirties were clearly serious threats to the Mexicanos of Lemon Grove. The school case illustrates more than the community's adaptation to the life in the United States and the mobilization of the network. It also shows the attitudes that prevailed among parents toward settlement and survival in the United States. Children were expected to attend the local school as a way of further adaptation. In fact, these children, the first generation of immigrant offspring, attended school and were socialized into a sociocultural environment far different from the ones their parents had experienced.

Thus, although the majority of these children attended only grammar school, they belonged to a cohort that blended U.S. and Mexican life-styles and outlooks.

As the depression ended the Californio community continued to rely on the cultural foundations established by the migrant generation. The depression had further solidified the family network both through the successful coalition against the school segregation case and through the mutual aid people offered to one another during this period of scarcity. Then in the late 1930s the community mobilized again, this time to protest poor wages for the lemon workers. Lemon Grove had become a center of Mexican labor, but this united action was countywide and included Mexican communities from other parts of San Diego. In 1938 the field-workers in Lemon Grove organized a union called La Union de Campesinos y Obreros (The Agricultural and Workers Union). Meetings were held in Lemon Grove and the union became part of a large struggle in Mexican communities in Southern California. Many of the primary actors were individuals who had come from the southern peninsula, but these folk were no longer immigrants—they were now settlers striving to make a decent living in the United States.

The decade of the 1940s brought new challenges to the families. By this time an entire generation of Californio children had been raised in the United States along the border. Although most of these families continued to maintain ties in Mexico where kin and friends remained, allegiance to Baja California now stemmed primarily from the experiences of parents and older kin who a generation before had created the little community of Lemon Grove. The cohort of the U.S.-born Mexican-American youth had attended U.S. schools and had become conditioned to many of the values of the U.S. society. Perhaps nothing illustrates this new allegiance as clearly as the response of this Californio youth generation to the Second World War. Although these individuals were tied to the border, continued to speak Spanish, and considered themselves "Mexicanos," the majority of young men old enough to volunteer joined the U.S. armed services. For the network this meant a further dispersal of family members. Although most men returned to San Diego at the end of the war, many had learned new skills and had been exposed to new environments.

New industry and growth in San Diego also resulted in dispersal of individuals from Lemon Grove. Lemon Grove had begun to change and by the beginning of the forties was no longer a primary attraction

for Californios and other Mexicans. New opportunities for land development and housing signaled the end of the lemon business and with it
the jobs in the packinghouse and citrus fields. The rock quarry ceased
operation and most individuals were forced to seek employment outside of the community. During the thirties some families had moved
into Logan Heights in the city of San Diego where a large Mexican
community developed (see Camarillo 1979). People were attracted by
the presence of friends and kin as well as by easier access to the city,
where a new industry—the tuna canneries—attracted Mexican labor.
The canneries employed hundreds of men and women and, like the
jobs of the orchards and packinghouse in Lemon Grove, brought
together many network families around Logan Heights. The canneries
were built along the San Diego harbor within walking distance of the
growing community of Logan Heights. Work in the canneries renewed
common ties and the Californios formed new friendships, especially
with other peninsulars, as in the past. Tuna fishing, shipbuilding, and
the naval base and aircraft companies flourished during the
forties. These industries acted as a major attraction for citizens of all
backgrounds.

Logan Heights was just eight miles from Lemon Grove, and visits
to the friends and kin who remained there was easy. The community
continued as a cultural core. Family celebrations were still community
events, and the families that remained attracted people from San Diego
and from across the international border in Tijuana, Mexicali, and
Tecate.

Although the forties were marked by numerous intermarriages
among the families of Lemon Grove, which strengthened the network
bonds, the problems of the thirties, the war, and the changes in Lemon
Grove itself fostered a new outlook among the younger generation.
The generation born in the forties was tied to the kin network through
the institutions that had made settlement possible, but these were no
longer rooted to the geographic base in Lemon Grove. Many families
remained in Lemon Grove and their children attended the local school,
but now members of the community were dispersed in other areas of
San Diego county. A conscious choice of environment and the desire
for better schools resulted in a further dispersion of the network. During
these years family network members continued to rely on one another
for primary relationships, but new friendships developed within new
neighborhoods and places of employment. In addition to marriages
within the network, *compadrazgo* relationships intensified between the

family members as this new generation of adults continued to seek out one another. Family ceremonies were multiple. Birthdays, baptisms, and funerals, bringing together the remaining pioneer migrants and their offspring with the new generation of offspring, served to further the existing ties of the families.

Geographic dispersion of the network at first did not mean the serious weakening of communal relations. The institutions that had bound Californios together over geographic space, through the mining circuit, were now at work in San Diego county. People continued to congregate in the community at the homes of surviving pioneers. The celebrations that marked the formal institutions of marriage and baptisms were family and community events. For in addition to celebrating specific transitions for individuals, these ceremonies reemphasized the bonds and the families that were part of a recognized community. This included kin and friends who now lived on the Mex-

Women of the Salgado Smith family in Logan Heights, San Diego, summer 1937. Left to right: María Smith, María Sepulveda, unidentified, unidentified, unidentified, unidentified, Dolores Salgado Smith, unidentified, and Guadalupe Salgado. (Courtesy of María Smith Alvarez)

Ramona Castellanos with two grandchildren, Roberto and
Guadalupe Alvarez Smith, c. 1947.

ican side of the international border. These were times in which the
family played an important role in solidifying and impressing specific
values and outlooks on the past and on the pioneers. Ties to the
peninsula and its heritage were now centralized in Lemon Grove and

the surviving elders. My parents and their generation were bred in the small town of Lemon Grove and their life symbolized important values that they taught their offspring. They considered themselves Mexicanos, but they were also American citizens, born in the United States, striving to make their lives better. Their move out of Lemon Grove served to place the next generation in a new sociocultural environment, exposing individuals to influences and decisions that were not part of the past. In the end the economic prosperity of the fifties and the sixties provided jobs and living alternatives not afforded earlier. The trend of a new era for the network had truly begun.

An important factor in the change of social relations during this time was the passing away of the elders. As the last of the pioneers died, communal events became less frequent. Celebrations continued to be familial gatherings, but individuals and their families became less and less tied to the network. Job responsibilities, educational preferences, and new friends influenced this new generation to begin shifting some of the alliances of the past.

By the end of the sixties a whole life-style had passed away. Lemon Grove itself was no longer a little community of pioneer Californios but a growing suburb of San Diego. Lemon groves and other citrus had given way to real-estate speculation. New developments in and around Lemon Grove brought more people into the town and contributed to diversification of the area. Mexicans continued to arrive in the area, but the community was not a focus of jobs. Mexican immigrants now turned to Chula Vista, National City, and Logan Heights, urban communities growing in response to the development in San Diego and the border region. The lemon fields and the related economy were forgotten. Today the only reminder is a large concrete lemon monument that marks the center of town.

My generation grew up socialized into two worlds. Lemon Grove and the communities to which pioneers had moved formed an intrinsic part of our social relations, but this was buffered by daily contact in neighborhoods outside the realm of the immigrant outlook. Schooling and other experiences fostered new values and aspirations that steered individuals into totally new life-styles. Intermarriages between pioneer families became the exception as individuals sought support from new matrices of social bonds created outside the family network. Only the celebration of wedding anniversaries, baptisms, and the occasional marriage continues to unite original family members. Funerals, especially of respected elders, have become the final reason for bringing together those people who lived through the settlement and life in Lemon Grove.

Los Castellanos in Logan Heights, San Diego, 1972.
Left to right: Tiburcio, Juana, Francisca, Narcisso, and
Ricardo. (Courtesy of Francisca Castellanos de Moreno)

– 8 –

CONCLUSION

When I first set out to write this book, my principal focus was the documentation of the settling of Lemon Grove and San Diego county by peninsulars from Baja California. I intended to show that the people I had known as a child and adult were strong, independent actors and individuals. Their experience seemed to fit the basic pattern of Mexican immigration, but it soon became clear to me that the settlement and adaptation of Baja Californios had been influenced by their specific history differently than had migrants from other parts of Mexico. On a general level the peninsulars were part of the mass movement of Mexicans into the United States during the peak period of immigration just after the turn of the century. The heritage of the Lemon Grove settlers was closely linked to the political and economic changes that determined the history of Mexico and the Baja California peninsula. This interplay, obvious as it may seem, highlights a number of important characteristics of this particular migration from Mexico, for it illustrates how interaction between individuals in specific social contexts produced strong social relations that became the basis of successful settlement in the United States.

The concept at the heart of this book is that the understanding and explanation of the settlement of Lemon Grove lies not in the crossing of the international border or in the search for jobs in the United States but in the historical process that was played out in the region of the Californias. Each of the developmental episodes in the Baja family network coincides with national and international political and economic patterns that affected the peninsula and human behavior at the ground level. When viewed locally, at the level of human interaction, the effects of these larger patterns demonstrate how individuals and groups of individuals interpreted and acted in the existing sociocultural milieu.

This perspective sheds important light on the process of migration and the development of social networks. Although these processes can be described separately, they are in fact intimately related as part of a large sociocultural process that encompassed and influenced generations of lives. Like the migration process, the Baja family network in the United States can be understood only by examining the particular socioeconomic history that influenced the decisions of migrants to extend and compose social relationships based on mutual experiences and a specific cultural history. The fluctuating economy of the mines in the late 1800s left little choice for those seeking economic security; as a result, the mining circuit population was forced to move from mine to mine. The development, however, of rich social relations stemmed from the geographic and social conditions of the mines in conjunction with the personal histories of individuals and their families. Internationally, the mines were products of economic conditions in Mexico that fostered a specific political posture encouraging capitalist ventures from the United States, Britain, and France. Together these processes illustrate how people in a specific region of the world reacted to hemispheric conditions imposed by the then current political and economic trends.

History here takes on different dimensions that need some clarification. In one sense, as in most studies of communities and groups of people, history is the background of the drama. In another sense, the California region's political and economic history exercised a specific influence on these migrants which contributed to the development of a specific type of sociocultural process. This larger influence and background can also become personal history, sifted as it was in this study through local behavior in the hometowns and mines of the south, becoming embedded in the sociocultural behavior of individuals. Each of these meanings of history is important in understanding how the individuals of this study were brought together, what factors influenced the extension of social relations among members of this migrant group, and what role specific periods of time played in the development of the community in the United States. An important element in this book is that history is not limited to any of these foci but encompasses their interrelations over a long duration of time, the *longue durée.* When viewed in relation to the analysis at hand, the *longue durée* illustrates the dynamic interplay of people and events in and across certain periods of time (see Braudel 1980:64–80). For this study history is more than knowing where people came from and more than a reconstruction of past circumstances. It is the incorporation of specific time and space settings that influenced human action over a long period of time, in human terms encompassing more than one generation.

The network described here can be viewed as a delineated set of social relations based on a specific history of experiences over a period that encompasses generations of lives, different geographic locales, and specific political and economic episodes in the history of the peninsula of Baja California and the border region of the U.S. state of California. This definition is not the usual type offered by network scholars, for it stresses (1) the importance of the development of a regional network of individuals and families sharing a specific history and (2) the importance of viewing social relations diachronically rather than simply as immediate responses to social conditions. The strong community in San Diego did not result from the better jobs and life-styles in the United States, although its being in the United States was a primary factor. The tight Baja Californio community was the result of over a century of interplay of people in an international region conditioned by economic and political processes.

The description and explanation of the development of this network of social relations is my primary focus. I have not been concerned with the attributes of density, multiplicity, or other linkage and flow phenomena that have characterized network studies in the social sciences. But there are a number of attributes of the Baja California network that add to current network analysis. The most obvious aspects of the Baja Californio network which distinguish it from descriptions and analyses of others are this network's binationality and its maintenance in the face of political barriers and geographic distance. This network was family-based and membership was culturally and regionally conditioned, especially in the early periods of development (see Alvarez 1985). The network's bonds intensified in a "foreign" environment and through marriage and kin extensions in the United States served to establish and reinforce family and town connections in the southern pueblos of Baja California. These characteristics demonstrate not just how the network was formed but how the people who have come from Mexico to the United States have varied. The network also reveals the use of traditional institutions in new ways to form viable sociocultural adaptations to new environments.

In addition to these characteristics, the network of social relations I have described draws attention to broader questions concerning the structure of social relationships. The network concept has been used to describe social interaction and the flow of socioeconomic benefits (especially in viewing the migration of distinct cultural groups to urban or urbanizing situations). The Baja Californio network, however, delineates distinct characteristics of network involvement indicating a structure of relations that extends beyond individual actors. Most network studies are ego-centered in that individuals are the central cog in the links and expressions of social interactions, social expression, and reciprocity. The network described here, however, emphasizes family and group membership based on regional and cultural characteristics. In a real sense this network is a sociocultural system that when viewed over time exhibits developmental changes that surpass both geographic locales and generations of individuals. From a migrationist's perspective the social relations of the network provided a stable set of sociocultural relations that inhibited drastic change while reinforcing communal ties and expressions regardless of geographic mobility. The existence of family social fields immediately provided membership in the network for any individual from families with recognized characteristics (such as southern peninsula background, experience in the mines, membership in certain extended families, crossing the border).

A significant theme in much of the migration literature is that migration causes the breakdown of social relations. But anthropologists examining migration from rural to urban areas have noted that social relations and communities do not really break down; in fact, people actually use traditional institutions to maintain solidarity and offer support to one another in new and different environments. Similarly, recent studies in the U.S. by sociologists examine the differences between social relations of people in urban or modernizing situations and social relations of people in "traditional" and rural environments (Fischer et al. 1977; Fischer 1984).[1] They argue that people have not lost community because they have moved to the city or because they are faced with rapid change in the growth of suburbia. People have developed different types of relationships, based on current needs and interests. These new relationships replace traditional types but are as qualitatively meaningful. To a great extent this creation of different types of relationships can be seen in the Baja Californio network. As migrants, the

Californios of this study fall into the homeless, uprooted noncommunity stereotype of migrants who enter the United States in search of better lives. The familial network illustrates that although these people were different from those who stayed behind, they were not the victims of a sociopolitical environment within which they had no chance of survival (except to return to the fabled land of real community). Instead these individuals, like migrants everywhere, left equipped with primary institutions that afforded the extension of social relations that became stronger as they moved through time and space.

In essence, the Californio social relations provided the basis for new communities and the extension of familial institutions, creating a continuing community that although not rooted in a geographic niche exemplified the supportive patterns exhibited in the traditional community. The "community" of Californios going north provided the support and relations that the "traditional" community afforded its members. These social relations based on the continuity of the historical experience provided the basis for the community in Lemon Grove. The community was the set of relations; it was the network as a bounded entity, discernible by its members.

Understanding the development of this network is crucial to understanding the migrant settlements in San Diego. At the heart of this process are the historical circumstances (or contexts) that conditioned specific decisions and adaptations among the group of families from the south. This is akin to the "constraint-choice" model used to examine the development of social relations (Davis 1985; Fischer et al. 1977; Fischer 1984). Simply put, people find themselves in particular socioeconomic circumstances that provide limited alternatives for socialeconomic survival. From among these limited choices people choose the best alternatives and create the social relationships that continue to offer support and social continuity.

Like the argument I present, Davis's model refines the notion of constraints to include the systematic analysis of history, power relations, the biophysical environment, culture, and demography (1985:8–9).

Included in these "constraints" are the geographic places in which the people under study find themselves. Fischer and his colleagues focused on the differences between urban and rural communities. Buttressing my analysis of the Baja network, in which social relations were developed in a variety of social contexts as the Californios migrated north, Fischer argues that changes from purely traditional forms of social relations do not in themselves constitute a breakdown of social relations. In the migration north Baja Californios supported one another, first through actual kin relations in the out-migration with family. As new contexts arose and people were faced with new milieus, other factors influenced their choices of social relations. These changing environmental contexts at the local level provided alternatives not possible in hometowns. As the social context changed from mine to mine, then in the border region, so too did the expression of social relations among early and second-stream migrants. Social life based on traditional institutions used in hometown environments were now expressed in new ways. The initial result was not unlike what individuals knew in hometowns, but now individuals and families were brought together into the matrix of social relations on the basis of experiences unknown in the southern pueblos.

Although Lemon Grove as a settlement exhibited similarities to southern hometowns, it would be a mistake to say that the settlement was the mirror image of the peninsular towns. People were able to settle close to one another; the settlement was geographically contained and settlers could rely on the immediate environs for economic needs. But this was a new social environment, not simply because it was in the United States or because it was a new settlement. Compared to the little towns of the south, Lemon Grove was a dynamically new experience for the Californio. This was not simply a hometown composed of townsfolk and families but a new set of relations shared among a critical mass of people. The network in Lemon Grove provided an unprecedented range of choices for social relations.

In addition to examining the processes of network development and migration, I have also focused on family life. My principal concern in this respect has been the role of the family in Mexican migration, both in depth and over time. The dimensions of family interrelations and the role of individuals in the family across generations and geographic space provide a clearer picture of the human qualities of migrants. The resulting description reveals how people deal with the specific circumstances of migration and settlement. Much of the literature on Mexican migration to the United States has necessarily focused on the large socioeconomic influences and effects on particular economies and host areas, but the individual characteristics of migrants are often lost in the descriptions. The family histories I have presented illuminate the human dimension in the migration process and aim for a greater and more rewarding understanding of family life in the past. The struggles and hardships, the affection and support, the determination and hope of migrants are not just individual experiences but a part of the movement north which conditioned perspectives and adaptive responses in migration and settlement. Understanding the relationships of families and their individual members through the migration process adds to our understanding of the family's relationships with the outside world. These Californio families were not merely pawns shuttled between sending and receiving communities; they were active decision makers during a period of rapid socioeconomic change in the western hemisphere.

The family histories of this study also reveal the complex nature of the migration process. The decision to migrate was not based solely on economic opportunity. Such decisions were made because of the economic and social support that kin could offer to family members arriving in the frontera from hometowns. The support of family was a primary factor in these decisions; not only did the family help in the move but the actual migration became a family experience. Families traveled together, providing security and support throughout the mining circuit migration and into the border region. Such migration brought together a number of unrelated families that shared a regional affiliation to Baja California. They shared the common recognition of specific hometowns with which ancestral settlers were associated as well as a common historical heritage based on settlers' long ties to the peninsula. These traits became the basis of a common sentiment that united these families thoughout their migration north via the mines and into the United States.

Mexican immigration to the United States has for too long been defined solely by the economic circumstances that condition the movement of people across the international border. The case of the Californios adds another dimension to these interpretations and draws attention to the variety and complexity of internal movements within the large immigration. Migration throughout the peninsula and immigration to the United States were the consequence of familial and regional traditions developed as the result of historical circumstances. The particular circumstances in the Californias which induced mobility were different from those in other areas along the border (although general similarities exist) (see Garcia 1981; Oscar Martinez 1975). The case of Baja California illustrates that migration, like all other human behavior, is not bounded simply by local, self-determining factors or isolated time periods. Migration in the Californias began as part of the sixteenth-century Spanish search first for a passage to the Indies and then for suitable ports and settlement sites along the Pacific Coast. These early beginnings formed part of the Spanish goal of finding the way not only to the Indies but to the Seven Lost Cities of Gold and to new Indian populations similar to those so easily conquered in Mexico and Peru. The result was stiff and often brutal rivalry between conquistadores claiming vast territories for themselves in the name of God and king. Migration in the Californias was thus part of a historical process that had its roots in the sixteenth and seventeenth centuries. The Spanish peninsula became oriented to the north first through the early explorations along the coasts, later through the search for the route to and from the Philippines, and finally through the search for suitable ports for the Manila galleon. This pattern of sea travel north was reinforced by the exploits of the missionaries in the interior of Baja California. The Jesuit chain of missions took a northward direction as the order planned a careful and complete conquest of the "edge of Christiandom." During this period Loreto, as the capital of the Californias, was the point of departure for expeditions and settlement parties into the north. The native trails utilized by the missionaries became the basis of El Camino Real (the King's Highway), which eventually extended as far north as San Francisco. These early routes continued in succeeding centuries to be the common access roads between mission towns, the frontera, and San Diego. The routes were used in all historic periods by migrants heading north and south. Travel between Baja and Alta California was thus a regional phenomenon and a basis for a regional tradition of mobility that commenced when initial contact was made with the peninsula. This pattern became the basis for a regional orientation of peninsular peoples which encompassed Alta California to the north.

The migration of twentieth-century frontera settlers was prompted not solely by this background of mobility but by the socioeconomic context of the nineteenth century. An examination of the processes that set the stage for foreign investment in Baja California and for the changing economic atmosphere on the West Coast of both Californias sheds light on the Californio migration. The study of these historical contexts further illustrates that migrations are only single episodes in a long chain of historical events. The family migration of this study is intimately tied to the nineteenth-century capitalist expansion on the West Coast of America and the rise of a laissez-faire political posture in Mexico, both of which provided economic alternatives for the families who migrated north at the turn of the twentieth century.

This migration of Baja Californios was no fleeting passage from home to host society but rather an important mechanism in the settlement of the border region. This was a stage migration that involved generations of lives—people traveling in coexistence, socializing their children together, and providing continuing support for one another. Settlers remembered the places, the events, the support, and the people of the migration as a significant part of their histories. Migration thus served to increase family solidarity and family relations.

The implications of these conclusions go beyond documentation of the Baja Californios who settled in the border region. This history of migration along the Alta-Baja California border suggests that similar patterns of mobility may have taken place along the entire U.S.-Mexican border, requiring the consideration of the entire Mexican immigrant and Chicano population with these network factors in mind (see Whiteford 1979). The great emphasis being given in the U.S. today to border control and Mexican immigration warrants the investigation, documentation, and inclusion of regional, cultural, and historical attributes of the border populations in policy-making decisions.

The case of the Baja Californio discloses the complex, multidimensional relations of the populations who settled along both sides of the U.S.-Mexican border. These relations were not solely economic, nor were they defined solely in the context of contemporary history. These relations were based on important historical episodes on both sides of the international border. Mexican migration into Alta California (the U.S.) is clearly a regional tradition that has been part of Baja California history since the sixteenth century. Furthermore, migration is multidimensional and encompasses both the self-determining choices of migrants as well as socioeconomic contexts conditioned by the interplay of foreign (American and British) and Mexican politics. Similar conclusions concerning migration from other Mexican regions are also surfacing (Cornelius and Diaz-Carredo 1976; Mines 1981), illustrating the need for a systematic investigation of the human factors involved in migration. This may lead scholars and lawmakers to a clearer understanding of any border restrictionist policy aimed at the people who settled and continue to settle in the U.S.

The principal viewpoint here is that of the migrant population and their descendants. I have attempted to convey this perspective because it provides a needed dimension in studies of the processes and dynamics of migration and adaptation. Without this view the importance of the family and its institutions in adaptation along the U.S.

border would be lost. Pioneer migrants identified significant institutions, time periods, and sentiments which help explain the specific migration and help recognize the significance of human actors in socioeconomic adaptation and cultural survival.

This book could never be a complete history of the migration and settlement of the border families who originated in Baja California. I have only outlined the history and the sentiment that initially drew me, as a member, to the challenge. And I have left much to be pursued. There are multiple areas and questions that warrant further investigation in the history of the peninsula, the nature of migration, network development, and the use of personal histories to relate sociocultural processes to social scientist and layman alike. First, comprehensive histories of the peninsula do not exist. Much historical work has been done, but most is of a segmented nature. Few histories concerning the socioeconomic or political ramifications of the peninsula have been undertaken. At the time of this writing, there were no thorough studies of the prominent Mexican historical episodes and their effect on the peninsula or of the historical interplay with Alta California and the United States to the north. Only one significant ethnohistorical study of indigenous life on the peninsula and historical contact has been made (Aschmann 1967), but there remains a wealth of information concerning the early inhabitants, the Jesuits, other missionaries, and the natural environment of the peninsula. One of my principal assumptions here has been that the peninsula was always a marginal area, but this view has never been investigated. What theological objectives guided the Jesuit mission in Baja California and how did this dry, scorched, and inhospitable land contribute to the philosophical, religious, and national thought fostered by the Jesuits? Jacques Lafaye (1976) has written an interpretation of the Jesuit missions in America, suggesting that they played a prominent role in the formation of a Mexican national attitude. The history of trade and mobility in pre-Columbian times and in contemporary periods has not received adequate treatment. My own investigations suggest that strong ties developed between particular gulf ports and that cross-gulf kin ties exist. Numerous Californios went across the gulf to Cananea or to Nogales, and many individuals have kin living on the mainland near Guaymas, Empalme, and other sites in Sonora. The gulf itself has never been viewed from a sociohistorical perspective. Studies concerning the entire realm of the frontera have understandably been contemporary (Spicer [1962] is the exception). But these studies have concentrated on migration and the influx of Mexican immigrants to the United States. As this study illustrates there is a dimension—historical and contemporary—that warrants a focused view of the migrant. Numerous towns similar to the towns described here exist along both sides of the 2,000-mile border. What types of networks have evolved as a result of migration in these and more northerly areas? Many Chicanos and Mexicanos in the United States identify original home areas and speak of kin ties in those regions of Mexico. The investigation and documentation of these ties are important to understanding the contemporary Mexican and U.S.-Chicano population. Other questions and areas of further study are multiple. Those concerning network development, migration dynamics, and regional affiliation might contribute to a general understanding of human behavior. Just as significant, however, would be perspectives taken from the actor's point of view in these processes. Since the majority of individuals who gave me their time and their histories were elders, I wonder about the untold stories of old ones who continue to make the peninsula their home, and of others who also lived through the times outlined here. The documentation and consolidation of individual perspectives into interpretive history is not only warranted but greatly needed. If I have done anything here, I hope it is to show that individuals are knowers and that as actors they can relate their own history in interpretive ways.

APPENDIX: ORIGINAL SPANISH FIELD NOTES

page 52

a.   . . . Primero cuando nosotros llegamos ahí a Calmallí estaba un viejo Ibarra, Don Emiliano Ibarra. Este trabajaba minitas de metal, pero como no tenia dinero, no tenia fuerzas para hacer nada.

Entonces Ibarra consiguio . . . fué unos Americanos de esa compania de San Francisco. Bueno, a Ibarra le dieron 25 mil dolar oro por los prospectos. Tenia unos agujeritos que tenia allí y el vendio (Loreto Marquez, 2/18/76:5).

b.   La compania vio que estaba muy buena la mina, y gasto miles y miles de dolares pa' mandar los barcos de San Francisco al puerto. El puerto se llama Santo Domingo. Ahí en Santo Domingo mandaron [the Mexican government] gente de allí de Ensenada, seladores y todo para cuidar el puerto donde llegaban los barcos y todo eso. Pues ahí tenia el gobierno empleados. Ahí cuidaban los barcos que llegaban a descargar las cargas (Marquez, 1976:5).

De aquí [San Diego] llevaban muchisma maquinaria. Pusieron un molino de 20 estampas en Calmallí. O movimiento grande. Pero, que barbaridad! Era muy costoso. De Santo Domingo, que es el puerto donde descargaba el barco, todo lo que traen de alla, mercancia, comida, sacate, lo tenian que llevar. Alla [Calmallí] no había nada.

page 53

Ahí del puerto . . . hay 50 millas, donde esta, pusieron el molino.

Yo no se como caramba, lo hicieron. Yo trabajaba en el molino, pero ya estaba puesto todo [chuckle]. No se como lo llevaron. Madera, comida, zapatos para los animales, tantísimos animales. Habian como 4, 5 carros con 6, 8 mulas cada carro. Figurate. Verdad. Pues ciertamente estuvo muy rico, sacaron mucho oro.

pages 61—62

La vida fué muy dúra. Pues en esos años no habia. ¡Uuh! Que ahora, que va, ahora [unintelligible] es la gloria la comparación. Y no solamente yo, pues mi familia y muchos que habia.

A trabajo salia. Pues, allí en el Triunfo, en ese tiempo pues, estabamos nosotros. Nos criamos en el pueblito de San Antonio. Esta cerquita del Triunfo el camino que va a San José del Cabo. De La Paz va el camino a San José. Ahora hay muy buen camino. En esos años no habia mas que de (pause)... nada. A puro pie pa' 'rriba de las lomas, a donde quiera, a ir al trabajo en la mañana, a qualquier hora, y llovia. Tenía que ir uno siempre.

page 62

Lo ocupaban a uno... afuera. No entraba uno, chico, adentro. Eran puros hombres grandes adentro. Habia mucha maquinaria para sacar el metal de las minas. Y aquí, por ejemplo [illustrating to me] a la banqueta [to the street—some 25 feet] era la planilla. Y allá estaba la maquinaria. Y ahi vienen con un carrito. Iban baseando todo en la orilla, asi [making gestures showing the location and the movement of cars dumping raw metal]. Con un carrito lo dompeaban el metal alli, la gente grande. Y aca tenian los muchachos, como nosotros. Tenían como 15 o 20 muchachos allí, y un viejo que nos cuidaba y que nos mandaba (a nosotros). Lo que nosotros teniamos que hacer era partar el metal bueno del malo. Lo que no sirviera lo haciamos en un monton [gesturing with his hands, showing how they picked up the raw metal and piled it into two piles], no ves? Y el bueno, lo partabamos. Siempre teniamos un martillo pá quebrar el metal a cierto tamaño. Que fuera chico por que en ese tiempo no habia mucha maquinaria pues, tenian que llevar el metal [to the smelter] ya quebrado porque no habia quiebra-roque. Nosotros eramos el quiebra-roque [laughing]!

page 63

a. Pues nosotros nos embarcamos en La Paz y fuimos a Guaymas y allí nos dejo el vapor. Ese vapor en que nosotros fuimos ... era el vapor que corria la linea de San Francisco, todos esos puertos hasta alla. Cada mes echaba un viaje. Pues hay nos dejo en Guaymas. (3/8/76:12)

b. De Guaymas agarramos un barco de la compañía de Las Flores, Las Flores se decia la compañía, pero se llamaban las minas, San Juan. Pues hay (en Guaymas) estuvimos como 4 o 5 días. De allá de Guaymas nos cruzamos el golfo (2/18/76:1).

La compañía de Las Flores tenía un barco, el que viajaban pues a todos esos pueblitos. Pa Mazatlan y Manzanillo y Guaymas y todito eso, pues para pasar la mercancia pa' ca' para la compañía pues, y material y lo que se necesitaba en Las Flores. Y el dueño del barco era Mexicano. Un tal . . . Pancho Fierro que vivia en Mulegé. Y era un . . . le gustaba el mezcal como agua (3/8/76:12).

c. Llegamos a Las Flores y de allí, de Las Flores, era adonde estaba la Fundación y habia movimento alli. Habia unas 4 o 5 familias, una tienda. Y allí de Las Flores lo mandaron a mi Papa al mineral de San Juan. De allí de Las Flores lo mandaron en mulas. Ahí llevaba a nosotros y todo el equipaje.

page 64

Pues llegamos a San Juan. El [his father] tenia trabajo ahi con la compañía. Un mineral arriba de la sierra. Era muy frio y uy! nebaba mucho ahí. Pues el era minero y lo echaban a la mina y nosotros nos poniamos afuera a limpiar el metal y a partarlo.

El metal lo bajaban de la sierra. Pues una sierra, que yo no se como hicieron ese trabajo. Allí en la compañía de Las Flores pusieron unos cables con castillos. [Illustrating with his hands] Aqui esta el cañon, verdad? Y aqui es sierra y aqui es sierra (describing a ravine in the mountain that enters the valley floor at a right angle) y por los dos lados de la sierra pusieron castillos de madera con un cable. Tiene como 2 o 3 millas de largo. En la pura sierra, en las piedras. Y allá bajo donde estaba (el deposito) allá llegaba al valle. Ahi estaba un deposito donde llevaban el metal.

El metal lo bajaban de la sierra en unas (que les decian) canastillas, unos cajoncitos de fierro. Aca, arriba de la sierra [still gesturing with his hands] habian unas ruedas muy grandes con el cable enredado alli. Y uno con un palo aqui (at the base) no mas lo tenia, pa' que no iba muy recio, porque los que 'staban llenos se iban muy recio por muy pesadas. Con esas jalaban las vacías pa' 'rriba.

Despacito, te digo, daban vuelta, vuelta y vuelta. Asi las llenas pasaban las vacias subian para 'rriba y daban la vuelta (2/18/76:3).

Ahí [in the valley] estaba la Hacienda (como decian) donde estaba la fundación. Porque era metal de fundación. Bueno pues ese trabajo duro alli, creo que duramos dos años o tres... como tres años duramos, alli en el trabajo, se acabo y se paro todo.

pages 64–65

a. Bueno, entonces la gente comenzó a salir pa donde podia pues. Unos salieron a Mazatlán, a Guaymas, al Palmar. En ese tiempo nosotros nos venimos ahi en la pura sierra. Pero no mas vieras las trajedias. Con puros burros. [unintelligible] Andaba uno para llegar donde habia agua. Nos venimos de San Juan a Calmallí.

page 65

De Las Flores fuimos a Calmallí. Y ahi de Calmallí, y acabo tambien, y volviamos a Las Flores otra vez. Pero entonces ya veniamos ya por tierra, battallando con las cargas de burro. Dos días o tres de camino para llegar a Las Flores, a trabajar otra vez. Entonces fué en Las Flores, ahi estuvimos viviendo otra vez, de vuelta. No se que tanto tiempo seria, por que el trabajo, paro arriba [in the mines of San Juan]. Allá en Las Flores había trabajito y ahi trabajamos (3/8/76:17).

Venimos a Santa Rosalía y de Santa Rosalía pa' tras otra vez. Ahí estuvimos mucho tiempo en Santa Rosalía. Hasta que ya que se paró el trabajo venimos a Las Flores. Y de ahí, de Las Flores volvimos a Calmallí otra vez. Con otra compañía que comenzo a trabajar poco de tiempo hasta que se acabó (3/8/76:17).

En ese tiempo yo tenia como, yo tenia 20, 21 años [laughing]. Yo creo que en Santa Rosalía cumplí 20 años yo [1900].

pages 65–66

Ni modo cuando nosotros supimos [about his father], yo estaba trabajando muy bien en Santa Rosalía. Ganaba dos pesos diarios [laugh], dos pesos plata [laughing]. Era un dineral.

En aquel tiempo era muchísimo. Sí, ya nos dijeron, ya sabian que estaba (mi papa) en Calmallí. Cuando acordamos, llego un hombre con 10 mulas. Porque (mi papa) el agarro muy buen trabajo y le pusieron de capitan de las minas, porque era todo lo que sabia ser el, las minas.

Bueno pues, yo estaba alli, poquiteando con mi trabajando. Ganaba bastante dinero para cuidarle la gente ahi. Mi mama y a mi hermana y al "Tey" que era toda la familia. Pues cuando va llegando el hombre con aquel ejercito de animales, que les iba dar? Bueno, llego. Ya lo conoci al señor. Antonio Espinoza se llamaba.

"Bueno," dice, "pues aqui vengo. Se me mando Doroteo por ustedes, pa' llevarles a Calmalli."

page 66

Pues otro día salimos de ahi, pa Calmallí... El otro día en la tarde pues, a empacar y todo.... Fueron unos conocidos (a la casa) hay estaban fregando. Era una bola... eee!
Victor: No querian que salieran de allí.
Sí, cuantos conocidos, pues.

page 67

Huele a vino y aceite de olivo. Comondú, el paraiso de ala, tiene un arroyo de aceite y otro de vino, que metaforicamente cruzan toda la tierra fertil de la hondanada donde se esconde el pueblo. Comparandolo con el eden... a Comondú solo le falta el rio de leche, ya que sobran Cascadas de datiles y torrentes de higo y naranjas (Jordán 1951:226).

page 69

José Estrada hijo y Ramona Smith c (casados) en San José de Las Flores el 10 de Noviembre de 1895. El de 34 anos, viudo, nat. de el Triunfo, albanil, h.l. [hijo ligitimo] de Jose Estrada y Presentacion Garcia: ambos de el Triunfo; *ella de 23 años nat. de Monterey,* Alta Calif., h.l. (hija ligitima) de Jose Maria Smith y Trinidad Romero, difuntos. [The latter are parents of Manuel Smith.] (Emphasis mine)

page 74

Bueno pues, ahi estuvimos nosotros (la primera vez) bastante tiempo. Habia mucha gente y habia bastante oro en ese tiempo ahi. La compañia puso un molino muy grande alli en Calmallí, una compañía de San Francisco. Gasto muchos de miles de pesos allí. Pagaban, pues, las minas, tres o cuatro minas que trabajaban... de oro, oro puro. No les costaba mas de pura asoge, el moler el metal y echarle la asoge y ahi lo agarraba el oro (2/18/76:5).
El molino de las minas estaba, o estaba retaradito, yo creo casi 2 millas o tres. Habia camino de carros, con puros carros con mulas. De alla la gente estaba en las minas y sacaban el metal. Y ya te digo con maquinaria. Con donquis, les decian a las maquinas. Jalaban y habian unos castillos grandisimos. Y sacaban el metal y lo echaban en unos chutes muy grande. Y alla de esos chutes venian los carros de alla del molino de Calmallí a las minas a llenar las. Y los llebaban (los carros) al molino.
De alli del molino ... yo trabajaba en el molino. Primero yo trabajaba en la escaldera ... donde usaban lenya, un trabajo de la

fregada. Levantaban el vapor para mover la maquinaria. El trabajo del molino ... si no mas, muchos no se dan idea ... es un trabajo, bonito trabajo y muy costoso. Muy costoso. Porque tiene mucho que ver. No, no mas de llevar el puro metal y que corre el agua, no! (2/18/76:7)

Y aqui en frente aqui esta, le dicen como ... un especie de chute donde cae el metal y un fierro que viene de la misma estampa, le pegue y de vuelta a una ruedita aqui y ya esta caendo el metal aqui adentro. Adonde pegue el estampa, no ves? Pero si cae mucho, no puede quedar mucho al mismo tiempo, no se levanta pa' riba y no trabaja muy bien. Porque el "estroke" de este es asi. Son 5 pulgadas de "estroke," no mas asi, de alto. No levanta mas. 5 y cae, y cae, y asi caen las cinco, casi al mismo tiempo.

page 75

a.   Pues allí en Calmallí ... muchos trabajaban en las minas. Pues por sueldo sabes? Y habia mucha gente que andaba no mas pa' alli pa' lla en las cañaditas buscando el orito, con unas maquinitas que ellos mismos hacían.

Bueno pues asi hacian muchos y asi sacaban la vida. Muchos sacaban, tenian suerte, sacaban chispitas de un adarme, hasta dos, tres adarmes. Las chispitas de oro. Y otros no, era oro muy finito. Tenian que usar asogue.

b.   Para allá donde estaba el molino quebrando las piedras, sacando (la compañia) el oro pues, estaba muy rico, muy rico. Mucha gente se enristo [succeeded in getting some gold] que no fueron tontos. Nosotros fuimos muy tontos porque no nos enristamos. No teniamos bastante inteligencia para agarrar ni si quiera un poquito (2/18/75).

c.   R. Alvarez: Entonces es allí donde usted conocio a Narcisso Castellanos?

Don Loreto: Sí, en Calmallí.

R. Alvarez: Ellos ya estaban allí?

Don Loreto: Eso no puedo decir, si 'lla estaban allí. Cuenta que ahi es donde los conocí. Yo estaba bastante joven todavia en ese tiempo. Pues tu sabes, cuando uno esta joven no se fija mucho de la gente. Si ... y trabajamos en las mismas minas alli. Castellanos, el viejo, Narciso, era mayordomo de las minas de los barreteros que trabajaban meramente las minas. Trabajaban como 15 o 20 hombres adentro, no ves? Era el jefe que mandaba alli pues. Capataz lo decian alá (3/8/76:4).

page 76

a. A Ursino? (lo conocí) allá baja en Calmallí. En placeres de Calmallí. Allí lo conocí yo. Trabaja en la mina alli con . . . (hay estaba tambien) la familia Castellanos, mi papa, todos. Habia trabajo bastante en las minas alli. Alli cuando yo lo conocí, pues lo miraba alli. Yo estaba muy chico y yo no supe mucho . . . como cuando uno es mayor. Pero ahi estaba. Llegaba a la casa ahi siempre, platicando ahi, como hacían la gente trabajadora. Pues, se juntaban en la noche a platicar alli en las casas. Alli es cuando yo lo conocí a el. Y despues cuando se vinieron todos los Castellanos pa' ca' [San Diego] el se vino tambien . . . siguiendo la novia. [Ursino wed Ramona Castellanos in San Diego.]

b. Alli conocimos a Apolonia. Hay nos juntamos. Yo iba al trabajo y pasaba como alli [pointing to a car about 20 feet away], como alli pasaba yo de la puerta de la casa de ella. Pa'l trabajo donde estaba trabajando yo en ese tiempo. Hay estaba Manuel. Adalberto. Adalberto tenia unos diez o doce anos, menos yo creo. Andaba con Manuel, porque Manuel tenia burros pa' cargar leña pa'l trabajo alli. Iba al monte, cortaba leña se la . . . llevaba a la compañía y lo pagaban . . . por cuerda y de eso vivian.

Bueno pues, a Apolonia la conoci mucho, ya te dije, a Manuel y a Adalberto. Adalberto siempre andaba pegado a Manuel. Atras de los burros [giggling] el estaba muy chico.

page 80

Alli [Calmallí] es cuando yo lo conocí a el [Ursino Alvarez]. Y despues cuando se vinieron todos los Castellanos pa' ca' [San Diego] el se vino tambien . . . siguiendo la novia.

(En San Diego) mi comadre Ramona trabajaba no se con quien. Pero no estaba casada todavia. Estaba de novia con Ursino.

pages 83–84

El estaba de novio desde que estaban allá bajo en el Marmol. Estuvieron tambien [los Castellanos] en El Marmol. El Marmol queda allá bajo de San Quintín en una sierra.

Yo no se cuantos años duro. Paraban asi de trabajar . . . y despues volvian. Una compañía de San Diego. Iba un vapor muy grande al puerto alli. Santa Catarina se llama, un pueblito donde habia un aguaje. Por alli pasaban los carros. Los jalaban los carros con mulas, desde el Marmol hasta la pura orilla de la playa, figuate. Hacian dos días. Si.

pages 85–86

R. Alvarez: Tia, usted no llego a conocer a los padres de mi tata, de mi tata Adalberto?

Tia Rosa [Rosa Salgado]: Ah, sí. A ellos los conocí cuando recien vinieron del sur. Cuando estaba yo trabajando con una señora.

R. Alvarez: Adonde, Tia?

Tia Rosa: Alli en el Alamo. Y alli llegaron ellos. Venian del sur, dicen. Llegaron.

R. Alvarez: Y quedaron (un) tiempo alli?

Tia Rosa: Si, quedaron un tiempo, porque el señor [Manuel] como esta[ba] trabajando alli. Uh! habia mucha gente trabajando alli en las minas. Y alli trabajó lueguito que llego. Trabajando alli en las minas. Y traía a Alberto . . . y yo tenia un hermano mio y alli estabamos. Alli estabamos nosotros, y Alberto venia muy joven.

Yo tengo un hermano mio. Llegaba [Alberto] el alli y le convidaba . . . llevaban burros. Para allá iban al cerro a juntar leña. Alla iba con el y traian leña. El juntaba y cargaba el burro y dejaba leña con nosotros tambien.

Venia esta . . . Alberto y dos muchachas. Una, María, es la, esta viva no? La otra hermana (era) Panchita. Egualita las dos. Y luego habia otro niño no acuerdo como se llama (6/18/76:10).

page 86

La muchacha no duro el año. Ya venia enferma, yo creo. Y fuí con ellos, la sepulcaron tambien alli en El Alamo. Tan bonita la muchacha. Tenia trenzas, largas. Hasta acá (6/18/76:14).

page 88

. . . yo vine [San Diego] aquí primero el diez [1910]. Mi hermana, esta que esta aquí, ella ya estaba aquí. Ella se habia venido de allá del mineral de Punta Prieta. Y nosotros nos quedamos allá. Yo y mi hermano, y mi mamá y mi papá. Pero no habia trabajo. Ahí estabamos en el campo, no mas (3/8/76:1).

Cuando se acabó el trabajo nos quedamos en Punta Prieta. Allí andabamos nosotros pa' llí, pa' 'ca, buscando cualquier piedrita por allí para poder vivir. . . . El patron nos daba lo que podia conseguir. El venía de Ensenada y llevaba cualquier cosita en el barco y hay nos sostenia. No se que harian con el molino, ya cuando desocuparon a Punta Prieta.

Cuando pusieron el molino alli, era de 8 estampas, no mas, era muy chico. Ya no pudieron trabajar, porque gastaron bastante para poner el molino. Cuesta mucho y bastante trabajo.

Trajieron un ingeniero, un alemán. Ese alemán era ingeniero aqui del Puerto de Ensenada. Se entendia alli con todos. Mi patron Brown, lo llevó a Punta Prieta. Y ese, el Aleman, puso el molino. Flick, se llamaba. Flick. Mister Flick, era Aleman. Grandote del carajo. Muy buena gente, por cierto. Cuentas que cuando ya se acabo se vinieron. El Aleman se vino pa' 'ca pa' Los Angeles, por alla tenia un cargo. Nosotros nos quedamos alla en Punta Prieta sin trabajo.

Cuando llego el barco de Ensenada alla, nos llevaba una carta para mi papa. El Aleman que estaba aqui agarró un contracto en San Quintín y queria que mi papa nos mandara a trabajar con el. San Quintín queda aqui, abajo de Ensenada (2/18/76:13–14).

page 89

. . . Pues allí en San Quintín, en unos años, no se cuando seria, habia un molino de harina. Una compañia de Inglaterra, muy rica, de un Ingles, vino y sembro, que sabe que tanto sacos de trigo allí. Puso un molino de harina alli en San Quintín. Allí levantaban el trigo y todo. Allí en San Quintín hay muy bonitas tierras, alli cerca del estero del agua. Hicieron buenas casas y todo, pusieron un tren, un ferrocarril con rumbo a Ensenada; pensaban llegar a Ensenada con el tren, para jalar la harina y todo pues. Para hacer el trabajo para jalar todo. Pues yo no se cuando esto sería, porque asi platican, yo no se, yo no estaba allí. Pero cuando nosotros venimos (nosotros venimos porque el Aleman, Flick, consiguio el contracto de levantar todo), decían que cuando estaba muy en grande, molian. Pusieron molino de harina y todo, y trabajo muy bien (2/18/76:14).

Bueno pues, nosotros nos venimos . . . el Aleman mando una carta a mi papá que nos trajiera a San Quintín a trabajar allí con el, ya nos conocia a mí y a mi hermano. Pues luego que abrimos la carta, no tuvimos nada que hacer, luegito mi papa busco unas mulas, los trajo y los dejo en San Quintín. Hicimos dos días de camino de Punta Prieta a San Quintín [chuckle]. En mulas. [RRA: about 192 miles]

Bueno pues, sí llegamos, luego con el allí, nos dio cuarto y todo a mí y a mi hermano para que trabajaramos. Y tenia como 10 o 12 hombres trabajando, levantando todo . . . desarmando, sacando todo.

page 90

a. El barco grande que mando la compañía pa' levantar eso quedo fondeada alla afuera, alla al mar afuera pues. Alla adonde estaba ondo quedo el barco, un barco inmenso de grande! Ese vino a levantar todo. Todito levanto. Y de aqui con dos vaporcitos chiquitos jalaban en pango, la carga pa ya. No mas hacian unos dos viajes al día . . . (2/18/76:16).

El barco se llevo todo la maquinaria que estaba adentro del molino y rieles y plataformas y todo se llevo en un solo viaje [chuckle] el barco, ya veras (2/18/76).

b. Nosotros nos venimos en el *Bernardo Reyes* a Ensenada. Nos quedamos no mas unos 4–5 dias allí con unos conocidos. Y de allí nos venimos aqui a El Cajon. Mi hermana ya vivia aqui. Ella era la casada (2/18/76:18).

Cuando nosotros llegamos aquí, llegamos a la casa de los Castellanos. Aqui vivía Narcisso Castellanos, papá de los Castellanos que hay de aqui. Ya vivía aqui en San Diego. Allí llegamos nosotros. Por que siempre fué muy bueno con nosotros y muy conocido pues, de allí de Calmallí. De mi comadre, Ramona, todos pues (2/18/76:18).

pages 91–92

a. Y a mi no me gusto. El trabajo aqui pagaba muy mal, muy mal pagaba. Que era un peso veinte-y-cinco al día. Aquí con la compañía, (has oido mentir la compañía) del distrito de agua que estaba aqui en La Mesa, allí haciendo sanjas a puro pico y pala. Por un peso veinte y cinco [chuckle]. Hechaba uno el alma alli. Y tenia muy buen trabajo allá [Baja Calif.] con el patron, el Mister Brown, que corria el negocio en Punta Prieta. Bueno pues, aqui no me gustaba el trabajo. Trabajando aquí, porque estaba mi mamá, mi papá. Habian venido aca ellos tambien. Despues de nosotros vinieron ellos en el *Bernardo Reyes* (2/18/76:18).

b. Me fuí un sabado a San Diego en la noche. Pues, quien era por mis grandes pecados, alla andaba (yo) en la tienda, cuando yo me encuentro, (mi patron el Brown tenia dos hijos hombres, tres hijas mujeres, y el mayor) el Kenneth andaba alli en las tiendas haciendo compras, cuando yo tambien iba a buscar zapatos, yo no se, cuando encuentremelo el alli.

"Que andas haciendo aquí, Loreto? y que?" dice el hijo de Brown, el hijo del patron.

"Pues nada, vine a dar la vuelta," le dije.

"Oye," dice. "No quieres ir a Punta Prieta?"

"Que voy hacer allá?"

"Mi papa va ir otra vez a trabajar las minas. Nos andamos alistando!" dijo. "Encargando el barco y va salir en tres dias, el barco, a Punta Prieta. Quieres ir?"

"Sí," le dije. Asi le dije yo. Que si. Y no sabia nadie aqui [San Diego].
Entonces . . . Y me dijo, "No quieres enganche?" dijo.

"Sí," le dije. "Como no."

Pues ahí vamos.

"Ahi tiene la oficina mi papá. Cerquita del Gran Hotel. Alli tiene una
oficina. Alli, vamos pa' 'lla. Y luego fuí pa' 'lla, lueguito. Y saludé el
patron, al Brown.

Y le dijo Kenneth, "Loreto va ir con nosotros tambien." "O, si. Esta
bueno," dijo.

Luego me dio de enganche $30. Pues riquisimo. En ese tiempo
estaba barato todo.

page 92

"Ay, oiga, Chicho."

"Que haces haciendo aquí?" le dije toda la historia.

"Ah! esta bueno," dijo.

Le dije, "Yo me voy a ir a El Cajon. Y mañana voy a volver y aqui voy
a dejar este veliz." Ahi estaba el veliz, el que habia comprado.

"Si," dijo. (2/18/76:19).

Buenos pues, te digo, me vine yo pa ca, en la mañanita, que me viera
mi papa. Y ooo! se enojo mas que el carajo . . . se enojó mucho. No
queria que me fuera. "No, me voy a ir," le dije. "El trabajo aquí no
sirve. Voy a trabajar con Brown."

Pues quizo o no quizo, ya en la mañanita el otro dia me fuí. Muy
en la mañanita me fuí en un trenecito que pasaba por alli. Y hay voy,
y asi me fuí (2/18/76:20).

page 112

Nosotros estabamos muy bien en Loreto. Y como Berta, mi hermana (se venía). Se habia dicho Miguel que se iba venir. Y dije yo,
yo no me quiero quedar, me quiero ir con Berta. A ver si damos con
Apolonia. Teniamos razon de ella, por el Senor Olagos.

Asi fué que venimos por aquí. Con el cuento que Apolonia estaba
aqui [Calexico—the frontera].

page 121

Trabajaba Olayo en el Lemon Grove, no viste esa piedrera que esta
allí? Allí trabajaba Olayo.

Levorio, mi hermano y el [Olayo] se vinieron. Yo me quede en
Calexico. Ellos se vinieron. El que mandaba alli, el mayordomo, era

Francisco Espinosa, un primo hermano mio. Y el los dio trabajo (Martina Mesa de Romero).

page 150

"Cuando llegaron los Franceses a San José encontraron agua buena y dijeron, 'Donde hay agua corriente, hay gente decente.'"

NOTES

1: The Historical and Geographic Background of Mobility

1. Today the town of Guerrero Negro, on the twenty-eighth parallel, is the only growing, industrialized section of the central desert. Salt is extracted there and exported worldwide. The coast was also frequently visited by whale hunters because of Scammons Lagoon, a grey whale migratory point, now a national park.

2. A *chubasco* in 1976 was the cause of hundreds of deaths in La Paz.

3. This is a shortened version of a paper that deals in greater detail with the personalities and processes of Spanish discovery, exploration, and settlement on the Pacific Coast. A number of references used do not appear here. These include Sauer 1969, 1966, 1963; Day 1964; Baegert 1972; Jordan 1951; Bancroft 1889; Clavigero 1937; Fagg 1963; James 1959; Mathes 1966, 1969, 1973; Leon Portilla 1973.

4. Cortéz's immediate actions after conquest were to send out his lieutenants to gain news of the western seacoast. "A distinct reconnoitering wedge was promptly pushed westward, chiefly to get news of the trend of the seacoast, which, it was still hoped, would disclose a shortcut from Europe to the Orient" (Sauer 1963:55).

5. Cortéz, set back in his plans to explore the Pacific, continued his quest northwestward on the mainland. In 1524 (following continued rumors of the rich Amazons) he dispatched Francisco Cortéz de Buenaventura north from Colima (Sauer 1963:58). Besides finding a large, docile population (and extending knowledge of the continent north into Nayarit), Cortéz de Buenaventura discovered the best pass from the plateau region to the coastal lowlands of the northwest. (The route of the subsequent colonial highway into the northwest was fixed for approximately 150 miles.) This route (used by natives long before the sixteenth century) paved the way for the first overland expedition by Europeans to the Colorado and into Alta and Baja California.

6. This monopoly had been granted by the pope in 1494 in the Treaty of Tordesillas. The line of demarcation gave the Portuguese rights to the eastern trade routes from Europe.

7. The Spanish zeal for discovery was again playing out its role. Once Fray Marcos's northern discoveries were made known, Cortéz attempted to gain the right to a follow-up expedition. Mendoza, then viceroy, succeeded in thwarting Cortéz's northward advances. He formed an exploratory-discovery partnership with Pedro Alvarado (an old fellow conquistador of Cortéz's), excluding Hernan Cortéz. Mendoza also issued a legal order (directed at Cortéz) restricting the incoming and outgoing movement of ships in New Spain. Cortéz was also forbidden to send a ship in aid of the Ulloa expedition.

8. The first successful return trips from the Philippines reached the California coast in 1543. Thereafter the Manila galleon began its annual round-trip between New Spain and the Philippines, establishing Mexico as a point of departure for the eastern trade.

9. During the first explorations and attempted settlements, a number of missionary orders visited Baja California. But all initial attempts at conversion and settlement failed. The Franciscans entered La Paz with Cortéz in 1535 and again in 1596 with Vizcaíno. In both instances the friars had no success in evangelizing or communicating with the natives (Engelhardt 1929:49). Three Carmelite fathers accompanied Vizcaíno on his second voyage and although conversion was a high priority they too failed. Between 1632 and 1648 the Jesuits had success, but these expeditions failed because of the difficulty of securing subsistence.

10. These sites were San Sereno, La Concepción, San Simeon, the Martyrs of Japan, Santa Agata, San Pedro, San Matias, San Ignacio, San Francisco Xavier, San Valeno, San Francisco de Borja, San Agustín, San Nicolás de Tolentino, and San Geronimo.

11. The royal license was given under the condition that the royal treasury pay no expenses without direct order from the king, further illustrating the lack of interest in California settlement by the Crown and its representatives in Mexico. Both Salvatierra and Kino were given permission to enter California under the royal license.

12. The other individuals were Don Esteban Rodriguez Lorenzo, Bartholme de Robles Figueroa, Juan Caravana, and Juan (a Peruvian mulatto). The Indians were Francisco de Tepehui of Sinaloa, Alonso de Guiyabas of Sonora, and Sebastian of Guadalajara (Venegas 1759:227). Two branches of Marquez are known to have populated the southern peninsula area and Loreto Marquez may have been a descendant of either (Harry Crosby: personal communication).

2: Nineteenth-century Developments: The Socioeconomic Context of Migration

1. Scammons Lagoon and later Magdalena Bay became a whaler's paradise around 1850. Ships entered the protected inlets and bays of Baja's west coast and slaughtered the easy prey. Throughout this period seals were also taken and abalone beds attracted Chinese abalone fishermen.

2. During the War of Independence (1810–1821) the peninsula escaped fighting, primarily because of its isolation. The aftereffects and the reorganization of a new government, however, did affect the outpost settlements and the already growing foreign involvement in the peninsula.

3. U.S. statements regarding Mexico's retention of Baja stressed defensive reasons. Without Baja, Mexico's western shores would have been totally indefensible. Control of the peninsula granted Mexico protection and control of the gulf.

4. Filibustering as used here refers to the actions of individual adventurers who engaged in unauthorized warfare against a country with which their own country was at peace.

5. Santa Anna's last outright money grab was the sale of Arizona and New Mexico to the U.S.; the exchange was known as the Gadsden Purchase in the U.S. Special American interests in Baja argued for the inclusion of the peninsula but were unsuccessful.

6. Indications are the mining laws during Díaz's tenure. In 1887 a new tax law aimed at easing the tax burden of silver mines (silver prices in the world market had fallen). The law exempted coal, iron, sulphur, and mercury from all taxes, and only a slight tax was placed on precious metals. It also set low tax rates on plants and real property and prohibited all other taxes. The law furthermore provided for special concessions to encourage new enterprise and lowered freight rates on mineral products that were to be exported (see Bernstein 1964:18–19). Also indicative of Mexico's high interest in foreign investment up to the turn of the century is the government's opening of the Mexican Information Bureau in London (1900). In 1901 the Convention of American Mining Engineers was held in Mexico City as was the 1906 Tenth International Geologic Congress, which emphasized the extent of mineral deposits (Bernstein 1964:50).

7. The American lead was the result of two factors. First, British and French investment had been cut off until 1884 as a reaction to the French intervention, and second, the U.S. was geographically favored. The U.S. had already made vested interests in Mexico, the capitalist expansion from the East Coast was ready for new areas of investment, and the gold rush of '49 had stimulated the philosophy of Manifest Destiny. New areas of U.S. settlement also needed various resources. Mexican raw ores provided this stimulant in many cases.

8. Descriptions of the land grant during the Juárez and Díaz periods are given by Bancroft 1889, North 1908, Martinez 1965, Jordan 1954, and Stern 1973, among other sources. Provisions in the contract stipulated that the company reserve one quarter of the land for Mexicans and introduce two hundred families.

9. By 1911 railroads and mining accounted for about 85 percent of American capital in the Mexican economy. Between 1867 and 1911 the annual commerce of the U.S. and Mexico increased from about $7 million to $117 million. The total investments rose from a few million dollars to about $1 billion. The U.S. had secured more of Mexico's trade than all of the European nations together (Pletcher 1958:2–8).

10. In 1873 the U.S. inaugurated ore import controls. A U.S. tariff law imposed duty on imported ores, but U.S. smelters welcomed even small amounts of Mexican ore because of their high lead content.

11. Railroads that would link the peninsula with the north had been planned by the major concessions, as on the mainland, but the plans were never carried through. Small portions of track were laid around San Quintín in an effort to link that port with Ensenada, but the railroad was never finished. Other railroads were small ore-pulling and extracting trains used locally in specific mines.

12. The Censo General classified sectors with the largest populations as *municipalidades.* In 1920 the designation *pueblo* included small and large towns; cities became the municipal centers. Hence Tijuana, a *pueblo,* had not yet surpassed Ensenada, which was a *municipalidad.*

13. A number of contemporary pamphlets published by the various promoters typify the extravagant propaganda. For a list of these sources see Barrett 1957 and 1965.

3:   The Social, Geographic, and Temporal Basis of Network Formation

1. *Compadrazgo* as used here refers to the relationship that develops through taking godparents. The relationship includes the responsibility of the godparents for the welfare of the godchild, but equally important is the relationship established between godparents and the godchildren's parents. This latter relationship establishes parents and godparents as *compadres* (coparents), extending a fraternal kinship between godparents. Being asked to be a *compadre* or *comadre,* as in the baptism of a child, is considered an honor and sign of close friendship and respect between adults.

2. Virtually all individuals were allowed entrance. I have record of only one family turned away because of illness. Crossings were so informal that some individuals and families were allowed to spend the night in the U.S. and return to register at the border the following day.

4:   Calmallí: The Mining Circuit and Early Network Development, 1880–1910

1. In 1905–1906 Nelson, along with G. A. Goldman, traversed the entire peninsula for the Bureau of Biological Survey, U.S. Department of Agriculture. His description of roads, terrain, and population are almost contemporary with the migratory period I am exploring and he gives an accurate account of travel conditions experienced by Baja migrants. The report was not published until 1922.

2. This important focus goes beyond the scope of this study but is an area of future research concern. Studies of migration focusing on return migration and readaptation in home communities are needed (see Cornelius and Carredo 1976; Mines and Nucton 1982).

3. These were identified through migrant and migrant offspring interviews and through municipal archival data on baptism, marriage, and death for the north and cape territories in this period.

4. The silver mines of San Antonio and Santa Anna were first worked in 1748.

5. There is some variation, I suspect, because the ranchos surrounding the principal towns of San Miguel de Comondú and San José de Comondú may or may not be included in the totals for these localities. The 1920 decrease can be attributed to the growing economic activity in the Gulf Coast towns and the growth of the cotton industry in the Mexicali valley.

6. This was one of the Baja mining economy support industries of which little is known. The wood used in boilers was *palo fierro* (ironwood). "The wood is very hard and heavy and makes one of the hottest burning fires of the desert. It was once used in the boilers of mining operations and is still favored by blacksmiths for their forges ... formerly one of the commonest of desert trees, it has been destroyed in ever increasing radii around habitations accessible to woodcutters" (Coyle and Roberts 1975:100).

7. There were probably more offspring, but I have found record of only two. Mulegé records of death indicate that María del Rosario was born in La Paz in 1865. There are no birth records for Narcisso, but his marriage to a Gaxiola, a family established in La Paz, suggests that he was from this area. In addition, offspring in San Diego identify his birthplace as La Paz.

8. Although the exact date of arrival by the family is unknown, the births of the children indicate a date before the turn of the century, c. 1898. The family stayed until around 1909.

9. This information was provided by María Smith Alvarez and George Cooper, who visited Calmallí and Pozo Alemán (just outside Calmallí). Sr. Villavicencio lived in Pozo Alemán and related the names of all these families when he learned that María Smith was kin to Manuel Smith. He knew all those families when they were in Calmallí together.

10. Rosa Salgado married Manuel Salgado, brother of Adalberto Smith's wife Dolores.

5: San Diego and Calexico: The Frontera and Early Network Formalization

1. "City in Motion" is the city's present slogan.

2. For a complete chronological listing of immigration and naturalization laws, see Laws Applicable to Immigration and Nationality, United States Department of Justice, Immigration and Naturalization Services, 1953. A. Hoffman, Unwanted Mexican Americans in the Great Depression, 1974, pp. 24–38, provides an excellent historical review of congressional hearings and the rise of enforcement and interpretation of immigration laws along the border.

3. The new policy drastically cut down legal entrances of Mexicanos. Hoffman provides these figures from reports submitted to the State Department in 1931: "Between 1923 and 1929 an average of 62,000 Mexicans a year had legally entered the United States. In the year the new visa policy was put into effect, the figure dropped to 40,013 and for the fiscal year ending 30 June 1930 the number had been cut to 11,801. Between July 1930 and 30 June 1931, only 2,457 Mexican immigrants were granted visas, a reduction of 94 percent from the 1929 figure."

4. La Palmilla was a point where steamers loaded cargo and passengers heading north. Small dinghies were loaded at the beach and rowed out to the waiting steamers. The trip north took about seven days.

5. The previous decade two sons (José and Marcos) had been born in Mexicali, and the last two offspring, Federico (1913) and Victor, were born in Calexico.

6. Travel and communication along both shores of the gulf is an undeveloped area of study. Contact between ports on the peninsula and mainland appears to have been regular, even large-scale. Internal migration across the gulf is an important area for future investigation.

7. Señor Olagos had met los Smith in Calmallí and Las Flores, where they became good friends. He was a customs officer and traveled frequently to the north.

8. Although los Bareño and los Romero did not go north as contracted labor (*enganchados*), labor recruitment may have influenced their move north. I have evidence of only one family individual

who came as a contracted laborer. If some were contracted, it was not given as an important reason for leaving the south.

9. *Palo blanco* bark was used extensively for its tanning properties. The missionaries used it, and many residents of the southern cape collected and sold the wood to foreign merchants. The local use and selling of the tree virtually cleared the Gulf Coast. Today the trees are abundant only at higher elevations (Coyle and Roberts 1975:88).

6: San Diego–Lemon Grove: Florescence, 1930–1950

1. *Mexicanidad* is Mexican national sentiment.

2. Apex families are not solely a retrospective view of the development of the Baja Californio network. I consider them important in forming other migrant networks. Latino migrant and other migrant literature does not mention such families, but the general treatment of mutual aid, reciprocity, and kin extensions suggest that such families are evident in other adaptive situations. Rural-urban migrants arriving in Guatemala City rely on apex families from hometown areas (personal communiqué, William Demarest, 1978).

3. Loreto Marquez recalled visiting the original Señor Simpson in a small house the family had built in San Antonio. Little did anyone realize then that thirty years later, after traveling and living in a variety of peninsular mining towns, these two families would settle in San Diego, almost a thousand miles from their home pueblos.

4. This was in reality a separatist movement supported by the Industrial Workers of the World (IWW), which planned to join the Mexican revolution and socialize Mexico for the Mexican people (see Blaisdell 1962).

8: Conclusion

1. Fischer's argument (somewhat simplified) is that the onslaught of modernization and urbanization has not caused a breakdown or decline of community as we know it. In fact, social relations in urban situations are as intense, as supportive, and as meaningful as social relations in traditional settings. The social relations of people in complex settings are structured like those in the traditional setting and to a great extent they take the place of community as social scientists have defined it.

BIBLIOGRAPHY

Alvarez, Robert R.
   1985   The Border as Social System: The California Case. *In* The New
           Scholar 9:119–133.

   1986   The Lemon Grove Incident: The Nation's First Successful Desegrega-
           tion Court Case. Journal of San Diego History. Volume XXII, 2
           (Spring).

Aschmann, Homer
   1967   The Central Desert of Baja California: Demography and Ecology.
           Riverside, Calif. Manessier.

Baegert, Johann Jakob
   1952   Observations in Lower California, 1771. Translated by M. M. Branden-
           burg and Carl C. Baumann. Berkeley and Los Angeles: University of
           California Press.

Balderrama, Francisco E.
   1982   In Defense of La Raza: The Mexican Consulate and the Mexican
           Community, 1926 to 1936. Tucson: University of Arizona Press.

Bancroft, Hubert H.
   1889   History of the North Mexican States and Texas. Vol. 16, 1801–1889.
           San Francisco: The History Company.

Barrett, Ellen C.
   1957   Baja California, 1535–1956. Los Angeles: Bennett and Marshall.

   1967   Baja California II, 1535–1964. Los Angeles: Westernlore Press.

Berstein, Marvin O.
1964   The Mexican Mining Industry, 1890–1950. New York: State University of New York.

Blaisdell, Lowell L.
1962   The Desert Revolution: Baja California, 1911. Madison: University of Wisconsin Press.

Bogardus, Emory
1934   Mexicans in the United States. Los Angeles: University of Southern California Press.

Bolton, Herbert E.
1908   Spanish Exploration in the Southwest, 1542–1706. New York: Barnes and Noble.

Braudel, Fernand
1980   History and the Social Sciences: The Longue Durée. In On History, pp. 25–55. Chicago: University of Chicago Press.

Bruner, Edward M.
1973   Kin and Non-kin. In Urban Anthropology, ed. Aiden Southall, pp. 373–372. New York: Oxford University Press.

Buffum, E. Gould
1959   Six Months in the Gold Mines from a Journal of Three Years' Residence in Upper and Lower California: 1847, 1848, 1849. Glendale, Calif.: Ward Ritchie Press.

Butterworth, Douglas S.
1970   A Study of the Urbanization Process among Mixtec Migrants from Tilantongo in Mexico City. In Peasants in Cities, ed. W. Mangin, pp. 98–113. Boston: Houghton Mifflin.

Camarillo, Albert
1979   Chicanos in a Changing Society. Cambridge, Mass.: Harvard University Press.

Cardoso, Lawrence
1974   Mexican Emigration to the United States, 1900–1930: An Analysis of Socio-economic Causes. Ph.D. Dissertation, University of Connecticut.

Carter, Thomas
1970   Mexican Americans in School: A History of Educational Neglect. New York: College Entrance Examination Board.

Chevalier, François
1963   Land and Society in Colonial Mexico. Berkeley and Los Angeles: University of California Press.

Clavigero, Don Francisco Javier
1971   The History of Lower California. Riverside, Calif.: Manessier. Reprint of 1937 translation.

Cornelius, Wayne, with Juan Diaz-Carredo
1976   Mexican Migration to the United States: The View from the Sending Communities. Migration and Development Study Group, Center for International Studies. Cambridge, Mass.: MIT Press.

Coyle, Jeanette, and Norman C. Roberts
1975   A Field Guide to the Common and Interesting Plants of Baja California. La Jolla, Calif.: Natural History Publishing Co.

Crosby, Harry
1981   The Last of the Californios. La Jolla, Calif.: Copely Books.

Crowe, P. W.
1978   Good Fences Make Good Neighbors: Social Networks at Three Levels of Urbanization in Tirol, Austria. Ph.D. Dissertation. Stanford University.

Day, Grove A.
1964   Coronado's Quest. Berkeley and Los Angeles: University of California Press.

Davis, William G.
1986   Class, Political Constraints, and Entrepreneurial Strategies: Elites and Petty Market Traders in Northern Luzon. In Entrepreneurs and Social Change, ed. Sydney Greenfield and Arnold Stricken. Society for Economic Anthropology. Monograph no. 2. University Press of America.

Departamento de la Estadistica Nacional
1926a   Censo General de Habitantes, 1921. Baja California Sur. Mexico D.F.

1926b   Censo General de Habitantes, 1921. Baja California Norte. Mexico D.F.

Divine, Robert
1957   American Immigration Policy, 1924–1952. New Haven: Yale University Press.

Doughty, Paul
  1970   Behind the Back of the City: Provincial Life in Lima, Peru. *In* Peasants in Cities, ed. W. Mangin, pp. 30–46. Boston: Houghton Mifflin.

Engelhardt, Zephyrin
  1929   Missions and Missionaries of California. Vol. 1, Lower California. Santa Barbara, Calif.

Fagg, John E.
  1963   Latin America: A General History. New York: Macmillan.

Fischer, Claude S.
  1984   To Dwell among Friends. Chicago: University of Chicago Press.

Fischer, Claude S. et al.
  1977   Networks and Places. New York: The Free Press.

Friedl, Ernestine
  1959   The Role of Kinship in the Transmission of National Culture to Rural Villages in Mainland Greece. American Anthropologist 61:30–38.

  1964   Lagging Emulation in Post-peasant Society. American Anthropologist 66:569–587

Garcia, Manuel
  1981   The Desert Immigrants. New Haven: Yale University Press.

Goldbaum, David
  1971   Towns of Baja California: A 1918 Report. Glendale, Calif.: La Siesta Press.

Goodenough, Ward H.
  1970   Description and Comparison in Cultural Anthropology. Chicago: Aldine.

Hendricks, W. O.
  1971   Introduction to Towns of Baja California, by D. Goldbaum. Glendale: La Siesta Press.

Hobsbawm, Eric J.
  1975   The Age of Capital, 1848–1875. New York: Scribner's.

Hoffman, Abraham
  1974   Unwanted Mexican Americans in the Great Depression. Tucson: University of Arizona Press.

James, Preston E.
  1959   Latin America. New York: Odyssey Press.

Jordán, Fernando
1951   El Otro Mexico: Biografia de Baja California. Biografias bandera:
        Mexico D.F.

Lafaye, Jacques
1976   Quetzalcoatl and Guadalupe: The Formation of Mexican National
        Consciousness, 1531–1815. Chicago: University of Chicago Press.

Leon Portilla, Miguel
1973   Voyages of Francisco de Ortega, California, 1632–1636. Los Angeles:
        Glen Dawson.

Lewis, Oscar
1952   Urbanization without Breakdown: A Case Study. *In* Contemporary
        Cultures and Societies in Latin America, ed. Dwight Heath and Richard
        Adams, pp. 424–437. New York: Random House.

1973   Some Perspectives on Urbanization with Special Reference to Mexico
        City. *In* Urban Anthropology, ed. A. Southall, pp. 125–138. New York:
        Oxford University Press.

Lingenfelter, Richard E.
1967   The Rush of '89: The Baja California Gold Fever and Captain James
        Edwards Friend's Letters from the Santa Clara Mines. Los Angeles:
        Glen Dawson.

Lomnitz, Larissa Adler
1977   Networks and Marginality: Life in a Mexican Shantytown. New York:
        Academic Press.

1978   The History of a Mexican Urban Family. Journal of Family History 3,
        4:392–410.

McWilliams, Carey
1973   Southern California: An Island on the Land. Santa Barbara, Calif.:
        Peregrine Smith.

Mangin, William
1973   Sociological, Cultural and Political Characteristics of Some Urban
        Migrants in Peru. *In* Urban Anthropology, ed. A. Southall, pp. 315–
        350. New York: Oxford University Press.

Martinez, Oscar J.
1975   Border Boom Town: Ciudad Juarez since 1848. Austin: University of
        Texas Press.

Martinez, Pablo L.
1960   A History of Lower California. First English Edition. Mexico D.F.: Editorial Baja California.

1965   Guia Familiar de Baja California: 1700–1900. Vital Statistics of Lower California. Mexico D.F.: Editorial Baja California.

Mathes, Michael W.
1966   The Pearl Hunters in the Gulf of California, 1668. Summary Report of the Voyage Made to the Californias by Captain Francisco Lucenilla. Written by F. Juan Cavallero Carranco. Los Angeles: Glen Dawsons.

1969   First from the Gulf to the Pacific: The Diary of the Kino-Atondo Peninsular Expedition. Los Angeles: Glen Dawson.

1973   The Conquistador in California, 1535. The Voyage of Fernando Cortez to Baja California in Chronicles and Documents. Los Angeles: Glen Dawson.

Meadows, Don
1951   Baja California, 1533–1950, a Biblio History. Los Angeles: Glen Dawson.

Meigs, Peveril
1935   The Dominican Mission Frontier of Lower California. Berkeley: University of California Press.

Mines, Richard
1981   Developing a Community Tradition of Migration: A Field Study in Rural Zacatecas, Mexico and California Settlement Areas. Monograph in U.S.-Mexican Studies 3. Program in U.S.-Mexican Studies, University of California, San Diego.

Mines, Richard, and C. F. Nuckton
1982   The Evolution of Mexican Migration to the United States: A Case Study. Giannini Foundation of Agricultural Sciences Information Series, bulletin 1902. Berkeley, Los Angeles, and London: University of California.

Mitchell, J. Clyde
1969   The Concept and Use of Social Networks. In Social Networks in Urban Situations. Oxford: Manchester University Press.

Nelson, Edward W.
1922   Lower California and Its Natural Resources. 1966 reprint. Riverside, Calif.: Manessier.

North, Arthur W.
1908 The Mother of California, Being an Historical Sketch of the Little Known Land of Baja California. San Francisco: Paul Elder and Co.

Ortner, Sherry B.
1984 Theory in Anthropology since the Sixties. Journal of Comparative Study of Society and History 4:126–166.

Paul, Rodman Wilson
1963 Mining Frontiers of the Far West, 1848–1900. New York: Holt, Rinehart and Winston.

Pletcher, David M.
1958 Rails, Mines, and Progress: Seven American Promoters in Mexico, 1867–1911. New York: Cornell University Press.

Romo, Ricardo
1975 Mexican Workers in the City: Los Angeles 1915–1930. Ph.D. Dissertation. University of California, Los Angeles.

San Diego Natural Historical Museum
1977 Plant Life of Baja California. Unpublished manuscript. San Diego Natural Historical Museum.

Sauer, Carl O.
1963 The Road to Cibola. In Land and Life, ed. Carl O. Sauer, pp. 33–103. Berkeley and Los Angeles: University of California Press.

1969 The Early Spanish Main. Berkeley and Los Angeles: University of California Press.

Schwenkmeyer, R. C.
1977 Climatic Patterns of Baja California. Unpublished handout for Baja California Seminar. San Diego Natural History Museum.

Scott, Robin F.
1971 The Mexican in the Los Angeles Area, 1920–1950: Acquiescence to Activity. Ph.D. Dissertation. University of Southern California, Los Angeles.

Secretaria de Industria y Comercio
1963 VIII Censo General de Población, 1960. Estado de Baja California. Secretaria de Industria y Comercio. Dirección General de Estadistica: Mexico D.F.

1963 VIII Censo General de Población, 1960 Baja California Territorio.

Secretaria de Industria y Comercio. Dirección General de Estadistica: Mexico D.F.

1971a IX Censo General de Población, 1970. Estado de Baja California. Estados Unidos Mexicanos. Secretaria de Industria y Comercio. Dirección General de Estadistica: Mexico D.F.

1971b IX Censo General de Población, 1970. Territorio de Baja California. Secretaria de Industria y Comercio. Dirección General de Estadistica: Mexico D.F.

Shipek, Florence
1965 Lower California Frontier Articles from the San Diego Union, 1870. Los Angeles: Glen Dawson.

Shurtz, William L.
1939 The Manila Galleon. New York: E. P. Dutton.

Spicer, Edward H.
1962 Cycles of Conquest. Tucson: University of Arizona Press.

Stern, Norton B.
1973 Baja California, Jewish Refuge and Homeland. Los Angeles: Glen Dawson.

Taylor, Paul S.
1928 Mexican Labor in the United States: Imperial Valley California. University of California Publications in Economics, 6, 1. Berkeley: University of California.

United States Census Office
1901 12th Census of the United States, 1900. Washington, D.C.: U.S. Census Office.

United States Department of Commerce
1931 15th Census of the United States, 1930, vol. 1. Washington, D.C.: U.S. Printing Office.

United States Department of Justice. Immigration and Naturalization Services
1953 Laws Applicable to Immigration and Naturalization. Washington, D.C.: U.S. Government Printing Office.

Venegas, Miguel
1759 Natural and Civil History of California. London: James Rivington and James Fletcher.

Villegas, Daniel Cosio
1955 Historia Moderna de Mexico. Mexico: Editorial Hermes.

Wagner, Henry R.
1929 Spanish Voyages to the Northwest Coast of America in the Sixteenth Century. San Francisco: California Historical Society.

Weinberg, Meyer
1977 A Chance to Learn. Boston: Cambridge University Press.

Whiteford, Linda
1979 The Borderland as an Extended Community. *In* Migration across Frontiers: Mexico and the United States, ed. Fernando Camera and Robert Van Kemper Latin American Anthropology Group, Institute for Meso-American Studies, vol. 3. Albany: State University of New York.

INDEX

Designer: Marvin Warshaw
Compositor: Prestige Typography
Text: 11/12 ITC Korinna
Display: Korinna
Printer: Maple-Vail Book Mfg. Group
Binder: Maple-Vail Book Mfg. Group